"This is quintessential Barefoot—translating paradise into words that give us "mainlanders" our vicarious thrills. His brain-waves must be laced with sunsets and coconut rum."

Mike Tierney, Atlanta Journal-Constitution

"Must reading on a dark and stormy night!"

Ken Picking, USA Today

"I remember Jethro Bodean didn't like to wear shoes either. But he never got to dive with the pearl divers. Manic depressives beware! This book may be harmful to your paranoia."

Rick Abrams, Sacramento Bee

"Some parts of the world are only fantasy . . . except when the Barefoot Man writes about them. Obviously he has been touched by the barnacled hands of the tropical gods."

Dan McDonald, Resurgence Magazine

WHICH WAY TO THE ISLANDS?

by

H.G. Nowak
(The Barefoot Man)

Daring Books
Canton • Ohio

Published by Daring Books,
P.O. Box 20050, Canton, Ohio 44701

Library of Congress Cataloging-in-Publication Data

Nowak, H. G., 1949-
    Which way to the islands? / by H. G. Nowak (the
    Barefoot man).
      p.   cm.
    ISBN 0-938936-71-9
    1. Islands.   I. Title.
    G500.N86 1988   88-2713
    910'.09142--dc19   CIP

Printed in the United States of America.

Photos by H.G. Nowak.

Illustrations by "Taurein."

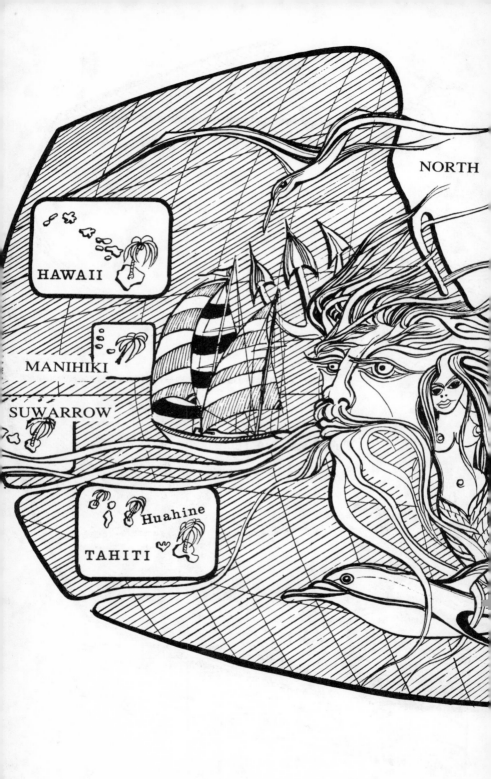

NORTH

HAWAII

MANIHIKI

SUWARROW

Huahine

TAHITI

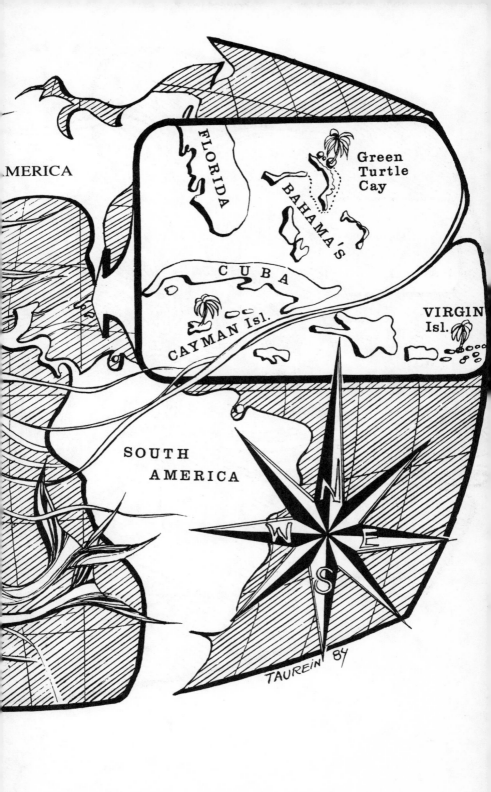

Table of Contents

Foreword

A native islander once asked me, "What is it with you? You live on an island, your home is right on the beach, you play in the water and sun all day and then you get the chance to get off the rock, and you head right for another tropical Eden." To him it made no sense at all. He was content with his little house and wooden skiff along the seashore. Well, I can certainly understand his contentment; however, trying to explain wanderlust to a person who is not moved by it can be impossible. Then again, I can try.

Take for example the cover of a *National Geographic* Magazine. Here is some guy standing on top of the North Pole, with icicles hanging out of his nose, eyes frozen shut, and blue-swollen lips. Yet he manages to have a victorious smile on his face. Why?? That's his thing, his dream, his wanderlust; he's found what he's looking for. And more than likely, after he's back down at a normal altitude and defrosted, he'll search for yet another chilly mountain to climb.

Mountains have never done much to whet my appetite for adventure. For me it's been dreams of deserted tropical islands with swaying palms and blue water hugging sandy shores.

That has been my dream for as long as I can remember. Even in my high school days, while friends were at the afternoon football game, I was at the library reading. The *National Geographic* Magazines were my favorite, and next came the atlas.

I would spread maps of the South Pacific Islands in front of me. My fingers would cruise like an imaginary sloop; and when I'd find an island with a strange name like "Manihiki," "Suwarrow," or "Raratonga," I would go to the index file to see if there were any books about my new discovery.

This wanderlust was probably inherited from my father who left my mom to join the merchant marines when I was but a tiny barefoot lad in Munich, Germany. Mom then remarried an American Air Force jet mechanic who relocated us (after numerous base-hops) to Wilmington, North Carolina.

As a guitar-picking teenager, I had a master plan. I would make a fast trip to Nashville, cut a hit record and then head for the tropics.

Well, fortunately (note that I say fortunately) it didn't quite work out that way. I did go to Nashville, with a guitar strapped to my back and a paper bag containing a toothbrush, a fresh change of clothes and a few original songs. But, three months after my arrival in Music City, I still had no hit record nor enough money to buy myself a Samsonite.

Had I made a hit record, my whole life might have taken a different direction. This is one songwriter that holds no grudge at being rejected over and over again.

I earned enough money sweeping studio floors in Nashville for a one-way Greyhound ticket to Miami and a connecting flight to St. Thomas in the U.S. Virgin Islands. Once I spotted the first white sandy beach and dove into the clean, clear water...I was hooked. I became an island addict; and to this day, I can never get enough sand, sea, and sun.

Since that first trip to St. Thomas, I've had numerous island adventures. Stories from these adventures and the characters I've met along the way could fill volumes. The fact that a full-blooded German is making a living singing Belafonte calypsos on a West Indian island is an odd story in itself. However, I have no interest in an autobiography, nor do I see a market for one. So what you have in your hands is a collection of stories . . . stories about my favorite islands, my favorite islanders and all the laid back, easy-going fun and adventure that has been a part of my search for paradise.

My guitar has been my passport. And I've never been fussy. My willingness to accept accommodations just about anywhere hasn't hurt at all, be it a lounge chair in St. Croix, a hammock on Bora Bora, or a mat made of coconut fronds in the Cook Islands.

There have also been many non-tropical stops in between, from recording trips to smoke-filled honky tonks, and even a performance in Las Vegas. However, I have always found myself back under a coconut tree, singing a tropical tune in exchange for a beer and a cheeseburger.

If you're an island dreamer like myself, if you long for sand between your toes, and warm tropical lagoons. . .I'm sure you will find some escape and some laughs in this potpourri of stories. If you have no sense of humor. . .best go buy yourself a good serious novel and put this book back on the shelf.

As a final note, I'm not going to apologize for the strange way I might make a point in this book, or my irregular . . . dots . . . Yes, the editors pointed these out to me. But, so what! I'm no James Michener or Herman Wouk. Heck...it's fun breaking the rules sometimes. Had I followed rules, my life would have been very boring.

Enjoy!

G. Nowak
The Barefoot Man

He's got sand between his toes,
And a sunburned peelin' nose,
Skin as dark as the rum that's in his hand,

The natives think he's weird,
With his sunbleached hair and beard,
Dancin' by himself to the beat of an island band,

Tropical beachcomber, Caribbean roamer,
Chasin' dreams and fulfillin' fantasies

From the Song TROPICAL BEACHCOMBER

NOTE: Some names, dates, and places have been changed
to keep the book moving along and to protect privacy.

Introduction

People who truly love deserted islands are a rare breed. They comprise less than 2 percent of today's tourism rush to the tropics. Consisting mostly of fishermen, sailors, skin divers and naturalists, this breed seeks what others do not. These people steer clear of high rise luxury hotels, rarely carry credit cards and seldom travel in groups. Instead, they enjoy the solitude of a deserted beach, watching sea birds nest and feed or engaging in leisurely conversation with a resident islander.

Barefoot is one of this rare breed. He lives a life of which most men can only dream. Christened H. George Nowak, he has chosen the stage name "Barefoot" for his band and himself. Yet, the name is much more than just a catchy musical handle. It is a statement of his personal philosophy and lifestyle. To his friends, Barefoot is simply known as "Foot." This in itself is rare, as few people carry the nickname of a human appendage. How many folks do you know with nicknames like thumb, nose or face?

I first met Barefoot through his music. I had heard rumors of a singer on Grand Cayman who had produced an album of diving songs called "Scuba Do." This had never been done before and, naturally, I was eager to meet such a man and hear him perform. I wasn't disappointed. The songs were remarkable, for they caught the spirit and excitement of diving as well as a deep appreciation of the creatures who inhabit tropical seas.

Since that day, ten years ago, Barefoot has charmed and entertained tens of thousands of divers the world over with his unique diving ballads. He has gone on to produce a second album known as "Scuba Do II" as well as a burgeoning collection of island songs, a songbook, a magnificent photography book and many other rich treasures.

Barefoot calls himself a beach bum, but I don't believe it. He is perhaps one of the most industrious people I have ever met—on or off an island. He is a fountain of creativity, constantly seeking new forms of expression. He is also a traveler. Some might describe him as a modern day Magellan who yearns to circumnavigate the globe in search of new island treasures. He seeks the undiscovered—those islands unknown and untouched by commercial development. His pleasure is to sample island cultures before they are diluted or destroyed by real estate development.

This book is a collection of humorous island anecdotes that portray the simplified logic and wisdom of islanders the world over. It is a collection of true life situations captured by a keen observer and told from the heart. Having traveled these same islands, I can say that Barefoot knows of what he speaks. All of it is true and without embellishment. This book is Barefoot's way of saying "Welcome to My World"—the opening verse of one of his most beautiful diving songs, "Planet Ocean."

Paul J. Tzimoulis, Publisher
SKIN DIVER Magazine

THE STORIES IN THIS BOOK HAVE BEEN INSPIRED BY ACTUAL EVENTS

HGN

Acknowledgments

Oh my...how can I do a page of acknowledgments? It's without question I will forget someone.

So I'm going to play it safe and just thank everyone mentioned in this book...and those not mentioned who read my pages before publication, passing on a lot of good advice...like Ron and Kathy Kipp, Susan East, Suzy Soto, Dave Martins, Carol Winker, Carl Gozur, T. G. (or T.J.?) The Councilor and...??? You see, I shouldn't have started mentioning names.

Then again, I have to mention "Harry" and express my gratitude to him for being a good sport, friend, the core of so many laughs, and a star in this book...

Can't forget my good friend, Carlton Lowe, in the Bahamas; Daniel, from Manihiki Atoll; or my sailing partners, Pop, Alberto, Dave, and "What's Her Name"...

...and Collins Publishers for allowing me to use excerpts from Tom Neale's book.

...G. Lee Tippin for the contact.

Oh gosh...Capt. Rein, from the island of Huahine, for his fantastic art work in this book; and Louise, for her tasty banquets in paradise.

Here I go...mentioning names. I know I'm going to forget someone...

Paul and Geri Tzimoulis for the super introduction ...thanks!!

Pete Gallagher and friends for the liner notes.

Hi Mom! Yes, you, too, for encouraging me to go seek my dreams...

And of course...my lovely wife, Geri, who puts up with this island-rover, patiently waiting for my wanderlust to end.

To the Caymanians, who have allowed me to make their island my home.

Finally, I am most grateful to the sea for holding a protective barrier around the many islands on this globe, for being so unpredictable, so vast, and so mysterious that many men dare not tread upon her...she's protecting paradise.

I

Initiation To Paradise

I was sipping my first ever Pina Colada at a small bar along Charlotte Amalie's waterfront. Between sips I counted the balance of my money. It totaled thirty-four dollars and some change. "Well," I thought, "this has to last until I find myself a job."

I had paid in advance for a small, inexpensive room in a private home overlooking the harbor. But before job-hunting there were some more important things to do.

First on my list was to explore. I could not believe I was here...on an island. I ate coconuts, ran on the beach, and dove in the clean water over and over until I would drop in the hot sand from pure exhaustion. This is the way life is supposed to be: the sun keeps you warm, and you eat right off the trees.

After several days of just playing, tanning and wandering about like some child in Disneyland, my pockets were empty and it was time to face reality and go to work.

I was not about to take on a job where I'd miss all those ultraviolet rays, so, I tuned my guitar and gave a shot at what I was best at...picking and singing.

My repertoire consisted of tunes by Hank Williams, Johnny Cash and the Beatles. Now, I found getting work as a country singer on a tropical island a bit difficult, to say the least.

However, where there's a will there's a way, and soon I convinced the manager of a small hotel that I could please his guests.

The hotel had a courtyard, with rattan-style furnishings, lots of green, lush plants and a bar, near a water fountain, that served those ever popular rum concoctions. My job was to stroll from table to table strumming and taking requests...sort of like those Mexican singers that serenade tourists with romantic melodies they can't understand the words to.

Well, this certainly wasn't anything that I had ever done before. My past performances had been in beer drinking, smoke-filled bars that allowed me a few numbers while the juke box took an intermission.

My first attempt as a strolling minstrel didn't go well! In this tropical setting, I was singing "I Walk The Line" and "Folsom Prison Blues," but my audience didn't want to hear Johnny Cash.

Usually some tourist who had no mercy would shout, "Hey, how about the Banana Boat song?" or "'Yellow Bird, Yellow Bird', you've got to know that one?" I sensed my new job wouldn't last long. And I knew my days were numbered when a hotel guest gave me a twenty dollar tip...to take a long intermission. When I got word the boss wanted a few words with me, I knew I was getting the axe.

"Listen, George, your singing is fine, though your guitar playing leaves something to be desired; however, people don't come to the islands to hear what they can hear on their local country music station back home."

"But, country music is real popular," I said.

"Yes, so is snow skiing, but people don't come to St. Thomas for that."

I admitted I was not familiar with most of the requests made by the guests. Then my boss dealt the final blow...I was fired.

The next evening, I stopped by to collect what little pay was due to me. There strolling in the courtyard was a West Indian in my place, delighting the tourists with his renditions of "Island in the Sun," "Jamaica Farewell," and "Yellow Bird." Though I was a bit jealous every time he received applause, it all started to sink in.

This was the tourist business, and a tourist would not go to the Hafbrau House in Germany to hear rock and roll...he's going to want the "Beer Barrel Polka." A tourist in Hawaii wants "The Hawaiian Wedding Song," complete with grass skirts—not "Your Cheatin' Heart" with cowboy hat and boots.

Yes, yes...that's it; if you can't beat 'em join 'em...I may have been a blond-haired Nashville reject, German country singer, but I was determined to learn my share of island songs.

I returned to the hotel evening after evening and studied every line and chord change of this tourist-pleasing music. I also noted that in between songs the Calypsonian stuffed his pockets with rewarding tips from pleased customers. That sight stuck with me...My pockets were empty and his were full.

I got my hands on an old beat up record player and some scratchy calypso records, and I practiced every calypso that I could understand.

I liked "The Mighty Sparrow" the best, though I had a hard time understanding his West Indian slang. He would sing,

Sell the pussy and bring home the cash to me,

I love you darling, but I can't remain hungry...

"What did he say?" I would ask.

"Sell the pussy, sell the cat, the cat," responded Frankie.

Frankie Jarvis was my landlord. He was a daytime cop and a nighttime drummer at Bluebeard's Castle Hotel. The best way to describe Frankie is just to picture a black Kojak, hairless head and all.

We would listen to more Sparrow:

The lizard run up she foot and it disappear,
Oh the children they searching everywhere.

"Hey, this guy is wild...I can't believe what I'm hearing."

"That's real calypso," says Frankie, "But if you want to please the tourist, study Belafonte."

I did just that, and soon I considered myself ready for the Calypso Hall of Fame. Frankie got me a job singing during the band's intermissions at Bluebeard's Castle...sure he's a nice fellow, but then I also owed him rent money.

From Bluebeard's I moved to the Pineapple Beach Club, then to the islands of St. Croix and St. John. Competing with the other island minstrels was tough; however, my price was always right. All I wanted was some food, beer, and a place to sleep. I made extra money from tips or lifeguarding at the hotels.

Somewhere along the way, I ended up performing on cruise liners. These floating hotels took me to the shores of nearly every island from the Virgins to Barbados. I was having a good time, but something was missing. My fantasies of playing Robinson Crusoe could not come to life on tourist-filled beaches.

I wanted more freedom, more isolation, and more sand without oily bodies.

Nearly a whole year went by, then in a taxi on my way to Charlotte Amalie International Airport, the driver asked, "Where you off to?"

"The Bahamas...Treasure Cay, Abaco..."

"Oh, is that your home?"

"No, never been there."

"So, what are you gonna do there?"

"Don't know...I saw some pictures of those places in your

local library, and it looks interesting."

"What? Are you rich or something?"

"No way, I can barely pay for this ride!"

With that, he left me to my thoughts. My first island experience was good practice for what lay ahead in my search for paradise. The mixture of fun, sun and rum left me with happy memories of the Virgin Islands.

II

It's Better In The Bahamas

One of my favorite discoveries is Green Turtle Cay, a small island in the Abaco archipelago of the Bahamas.

A big, black, Bahamian bartender at Abaco's Treasure Cay Resort led me to it.

"Hey, man...dis place is for you," he said. "It right across da sea der."

"Where?" I asked looking over the crystalline water.

"Dat way...maybe ten mile or so. Green Turtle a very small island...people dey fish and life is slow," he went on to explain.

"Are there any hotels?" I asked.

"Don' know man," he said, as he mixed another rum punch for a thirsty customer.

"Is it a big island?"

"No...maybe two, maybe three mile long...only four hundred people live der."

Treasure Cay Resort was certainly not the spot I was looking for. It's okay for someone looking for a championship golf course, deep sea charter fishing, and real estate folks offering free island tours. But for myself, the sign in the hotel lobby was enough to convince this beachcomber he was on the wrong island:

JACKETS AND SHOES REQUIRED FOR DINNER
RESERVATIONS PLEASE
Your Maitre d' JEAN-CLAUDE

Shoes were one thing, but jackets and Jean-Claude...I'm checking out.

The following morning I went to Green Turtle Cay. As the ferry neared the dock, I could not believe what I was seeing. It was too beautiful, sort of like a child's doll town. Small, brightly painted houses, bordered with white picket fences, lots of flowers, and wooden fishing boats in colors of blue, green and yellow lined the beach. Children fished along the shore, while the elders cleaned conch and repaired fishing nets. The sky was blue, and the sun was hot; and I had just found heaven.

As I walked down the narrow road, I could not help but wonder why a lovely place like this hadn't been ruined. It's only a short hop from Miami. My thoughts were interrupted by the sound of country music...live country music. I followed the sound, passing smiling, giggling Bahamian children who I'm sure were wondering about this barefooted stranger.

A small crowd was gathered by the window of an old wooden house; inside were a few locals, strumming a banjo and guitar singing a Jim Reeves classic, "He'll Have to Go."

"What's going on?" I asked a neatly dressed fellow standing next to me.

"It's a 'oliday comin' up soon; they practicing for a big dance."

"Hi, my name's George, and you are?"

With a shy look, he said "Carlton Lowe," scanning the crowd to see who might be watching the introduction.

"Hey, Carlton, where can I get a cold beer?"

This question turned several heads, and I sensed I'd said something wrong.

"It's Sunday and the Blue Bee is closed," said Carlton.

"The Blue Bee...what's that?"

"The bar," he explained.

I could see that Carlton spent a lot of time outdoors. He

was well-tanned, his lips were cracked and his nose sun-burned and peeling. He looked like he was in his early twenties and was extremely neatly dressed—bermuda shorts and white shirt, complete with socks and spit-shined shoes. Not one strand of his partially sun-bleached hair was out of place.

It was a hot May day, and I was thirsty. Almost whispering, Carlton said, "Maybe you can get beer at the Club."

"Let's go," I responded immediately. An instant later we were off in his speed boat, shooting over the glassy calm waters toward the north end of the island.

Green Turtle Cay has a low, hilly profile. Its shoreline is a mixture of jagged coral, sandy coves, and dense mangroves. It's about three miles long and maybe half a mile wide, making it a perfect little island.

"What do you do around here, Carlton?"

"Crawfish," he said.

"You mean lobster, don't you?"

"No, I mean crawfish."

Carlton explained that the spiny, clawless creatures found in these tropical waters, which I'd known as "lobster," were called "crawfish" here in the Bahamas.

"That's all you do eight hours a day? Go out in this beautiful water and fish for lobster...I mean crawfish? And you make enough money to buy a neat boat like this?"

"No, I only work three hours a day to make enough money to buy a boat like this," Carlton answered.

This intrigued me beyond my wildest imagination. "What a life!"

At the club we found cold beer. "The Club," as it's known to the locals, in reality is the Green Turtle Cay Yacht Club. The Club rented a few cottages and offered tie up facilities for passing yachts. There was also a small pub and restaurant that could seat about fifty.

"Where do you come from?" asked Carlton.

"Well, I've been island hopping for the last year."

With some surprise Carlton asked, "Oh, in the Bahamas?"

"No, this is my first time in the Bahamas. I've been play-ing music down in the Virgin Islands, Barbados, An-tigua...around that area."

" 'ow come you didn't sing a few songs back in the village?"

I tried to think up a reasonable excuse when a short, stocky, hairy bodied gentlemen wearing a monocle and sip-ping a glass of white wine appeared.

"Carlton, old chap, you haven't seen Roger dashing about have you?" he queried.

"No, sir."

"Well, cheerio then." And, as fast as he made his ap-pearance, he was gone again.

"Who's that?" I asked.

"That's Mr. Charlesworth...the man who owns this place...he's rich," added Carlton.

"Oh yeah? I wonder if he's rich enough to hire a singer for his little pub?"

"You best ask Roger 'bout that."

"Roger...who is he?"

"He's Charlesworth's son-in-law and the manager 'ere."

I thought no more about it until a young, handsome Englishman whisked by us. He made a quick u-turn and approached.

"Carlton, by any chance have you seen that father-in-law of mine?"

Carlton pointed in the direction that Roger had just come from.

"Cheers," acknowledged Roger. He was about to walk away, when I said, "Excuse me, sir...my name is George Nowak. I'm a musician. I just finished a big tour in some of the other Caribbean islands, and I'm on my way to

Nashville for some recording. (I exaggerated a little.) Well, I was wondering if you might be interested in some live music?"

"Oh we're just too small to hire a musician," said Roger.

"You don't have to pay me. Some beer, a lounge chair to sleep on and a cheeseburger every now and then is all I need. Besides that, I only have a few weeks before my recording session; then my manager will be looking for me," I lied that time, hoping to impress Roger.

Roger chewed on the plastic ear loop of his sunglasses and looked me over. I was about to make up another tale when he said, "Okay, come have dinner with us and let's hear what you can do."

As we walked back toward the boat dock, I had a victorious smile on my face. I couldn't believe my good fortune. Not only had I made a friend in this little paradise, but I had possibly landed a job.

My performance that evening went well. There were only a dozen or so guests; and if I didn't know the song, I made up the words. I was determined to impress Roger so I could stick around awhile.

Roger was a short, slim Londoner with dark hair and several gold-capped teeth. He was never in one place for very long—like a hummingbird, he was always moving. And was he smart! Once I got to know him, I thought he was the most clever man on earth. He could fix anything—from the generator that gave power to the Club, to the power saw he used to build the Club. He was a pilot, a boat captain, and an accountant. Roger was always working, always attuned to what was going on around him. He ran the Green Turtle Club as if he owned it.

The following morning, after a successful audition, Roger invited me to stay on a while.

"However, Mate," Roger reminded me, "We cannot pay

you. Help yourself to all the beer you like. You can use the boats and have your meals in the dining room, but DO NOT WORK...DO NOT LIFT A FINGER!" He had to say no more; I caught on immediately.

Though I'd spent less than a year roaming around the West Indies, I knew it was the same everywhere for a foreigner. In fact, it's stamped right in your passport when you arrive: THE HOLDER OF THIS PASSPORT MAY NOT WORK IN GAINFUL OCCUPATION. But still, I was amused that the first orders from my new boss were "DO NOT WORK!" Only in paradise!

After a few days at the Club, Carlton finally made a reappearance.

"Would you like to go crawfishing?" he asked.

"You mean lobstering?" I tried to joke.

Straight-faced Carlton awaited an answer.

"Crawfishing! Let's go!"

As Green Turtle Cay disappeared behind us, Carlton scanned the gin clear waters.

"What are you looking for?" I shouted over the engine's noise. "Crawfish...not lobster," he said, adding a rare smile.

"What? Do they float?"

"No, they in the drums."

"Drums?" Now I was really confused.

" 'old on," he shouted, as he put his boat in a spin leaving a circle of white foam behind us. He cut off the engine and tossed out the anchor. "There, see that dark spot on the bottom?"

I looked in the direction of his pointed finger.

"That's a drum," said Carlton. "Now put on this mask, fins, and take this shooter...now bring back some crawfish."

"Drum?" Still confused, I put on the gear.

Carlton handed me the shooter (also known as a Hawaiian sling) and gave me a fast lesson on how to use this contraption that looked like a cross between a bow and arrow and a slingshot.

"How deep is it, Carlton?"

"Not too deep—the tide low, maybe fifteen, twenty feet."

With the grace of a hippo, I dove in, almost losing mask and shorts in the process. There lying in the turtle grass was a rusty hole-filled fifty gallon oil "drum."

When I made my first descent, I saw what looked like hundreds of antennae moving back and forth. And that's just what they were...crawfish antennae or "whips" as the Bahamians call them.

Wow! I had never seen so many lobster. In fact, this was the first time I had ever seen a real live lobster in the water and the first time I had ever tried spearing one. Clumsily, I drew back the spear...Bull's-eye! Right into the side of the oil drum!

With spear firmly stuck, I came back to the surface for air. Carlton's eagle eyes had already spotted what had happened. He dove in to fetch as many lobster as he could before the spiny critters made their escape. Carlton managed to get about a dozen or so nice sized ones while I looked on, not knowing what to do. I had learned my first lesson in crawfishing...SHOOT THE CRAWFISH, NOT THE "DRUM"!

We stopped at a few more drums, and soon Carlton had well over a hundred lobster in his boat. I claimed one kill.

On our way back to Green Turtle, Carlton again scanned the ocean. Watching him, I could not help but admire his knowledge of these waters.

Then he saw something.

"What is it, Carlton?"

"There 'bout 'alfway from the bow to the beach."

As I tried my darndest to see what Carlton saw, he grabbed a long, flimsy stick with three pointed prongs at one end. He drew the spear back and let go. In an instant, the clear water turned red from the blood of a large fish he had pierced. Now, if I was to say I was impressed and excited, I would be putting it very mildly. This was unbelievable. It was like all the adventure films and *National Geographic* pages I've seen, unfolding in front of me...This was real.

Carlton now was not only my friend, but he instantly became a hero. He was doing what I wanted to do...cruise around in a boat, spear fish for his dinner, and of course, best of all...live on a small, tropical island. Yes, my friends, this is the life! Carlton's biggest worry for the rest of the day was whether he should have fresh fish or fresh lobster for his evening meal.

It didn't take too long to absorb everything that Carlton taught me. In no time at all, I knew every cove, coral rock, and coconut tree on the many small islands that were but swimming distance from Green Turtle.

I stayed on at the Green Turtle Club all that summer and into the early fall, canceling my fictional recording sessions.

My evenings were spent singing island melodies in the Club's bar and my days exploring and playing in the sun.

Abaco is made up of two main boomerang-shaped islands, Great Abaco and Little Abaco. Off their eastern shore lie numerous small islands or "cays" (pronounced "keys"). Most are uninhabited; the populated ones usually consist of a small fishing village or two. The people are descendants of slaves, British loyalists and shipwreck victims.

The cays are just what I had imagined tropical deserted islands should look like. Most have powdery white beaches, coconut trees and plenty of coral gardens in the surrounding waters.

"THE SHARK"

The waters around the Abaco area offer an abundance of marine life. Lobsters, grouper, snappers, dolphins, barracuda and...SHARKS...

Sharks are great eating although most Bahamians don't agree. Besides their tasty fillets, tourists love buying shark's teeth. Discovering that one shark's jaw would sell for twenty or thirty dollars, I soon started a little side business.

On regular occasions, just as the sun was setting, I would head for the ocean side of Green Turtle Cay and set my shark trap. This was a little contraption consisting of a cement block with a long piece of nylon ski rope tied to it. At the end of the ski rope, I attached a bit of small chain leader and the largest hook I could find. I'd bait it with a snapper head or whatever was available and drop it on the sandy bottom. Nine out of ten times, I'd have a shark the following morning.

One morning, I had pulled in a rather large fellow. It was a tiger shark well over ten feet long. By now I had learned that when a shark was more than four or five feet long, the meat was not too tasty. However, this shark's large jaws were bound to bring more than the usual earnings, so with the help of Alexander, the Club's all around Bahamian handyman, I pulled my catch up on the main boat dock.

It was still early a.m. so before starting my dissecting, I went to the clubhouse for breakfast. With coffee and conversation, time went by fast. Soon it was close to ten, and the morning ferry was scheduled to pick up guests for the regular airport run.

Alexander, acting as bellman, was wheelbarrowing luggage to the dock, while I was still jabbering. Figuring the shark was long gone to fish heaven, Alexander stacked the baggage around the enormous creature.

As the ferry slowly made its way towards the dock, departing guests were taking last minute photos of the man-eater.

"George...George...where the bloody hell is George?"

"In here, Roger, in the dining room."

With fury in his eyes and steam coming from his nostrils Roger commanded, "I need to have a word with you in the kitchen...NOW!"

I excused myself wondering what was eating him this morning.

"Get that bloody fish off the dock at once," he snarled.

"But...but..."

"No 'buts'...STRAIGHT AWAY!"

With that order the pots almost fell off the kitchen wall. I knew he wasn't joking, but I felt I had to attempt to brighten him up before he stormed out the back door.

"Hey, Roger...can I finish my coffee?"

"YOU CHEEKY SOD!" he snapped back, and he slammed a battered screen door behind him.

Pacing toward the dock to obey the order, I quickly came to realize why Roger was boiling. My shark had come back to life...only for a few moments, but long enough to create panic, hysteria and total mass confusion amongst departing guests.

One of these departing guests, a Mr. Thompson from Green Bay, Wisconsin, was hanging over the dock's side in sheer terror. Some flying luggage had just missed his sunburned forehead before promptly landing with a "splash."

While Mr. Thompson threatened to sue, Mrs. Thompson roared with laughter. I dove in the water to retrieve a few Samsonites—they float—and the ferryboat captain was already on his C.B. radio broadcasting the morning's events to everyone in the village.

I figured this whole incident would result in a one-way

ticket back to America. However, I was let off with just a harsh scolding from Roger plus a "What a bloody mess you caused!" from Mr. Charlesworth.

I dumped the menacing shark carcass back in the sea and disappeared to the surrounding mangroves where I went to work removing the jaws. I left the remains for the little sea creatures to finish. Oh what a mistake...why would they eat that big nasty shark that within twenty-four hours started its smelly task of decomposing? The tide managed to carry the carcass deep into the tangling fingers of the mangroves, but incoming trade winds helped dissipate a very unpleasant aroma. What was normally clean, fresh, floral-scented air turned putrid from the smell of 350 pounds of rotting shark. The north end of Green Turtle Cay smelled like some garbage dump in Gary, Indiana.

Several evenings following the big dock incident, guests were starting to complain, and though I had made several attempts to find the shark, it was all in vain. Then the wind shifted, and I had hoped all would be forgotten. It was...until Alexander started complaining.

"You best get dat shark from da mangroves or folks in da village gon get vex."

"Come on, Alexander...I don't smell a thing."

"Da wind shift to da sout', and if it keep up, soon scent be in da village."

Alexander always reminded me of a black "Lurch" from the old "Adams Family" television show. And if big, powerful Alexander said he smelled something, you didn't argue with him.

It was important to keep peace with the villagers; if they didn't show for work, the club could be crippled. No maids, no bartenders, no kitchen staff...need I say more?

Mr. Charlesworth then tracked me down; in his typical calm British manner, he said, "Mate, I'd like to chat with you a bit, after you find that bloody shark and haul it out to sea."

I finally found the remains. It was a smelly, stomach-turning task; however with machete, mask and fins, half a day later the decaying mess was dumped several miles off Green Turtle Cay.

Even after a lot of soap and scrubbing, the shark scent still stayed with me. I put on a clean shirt anyway and took a rare walk up the hill to Mr. Charlesworth's house. With tail tucked between my legs, I knocked on his door.

"Yes, who is it?"

"It's me, sir...did you want to see me?"

"Where's the shark?" he asked, without making an appearance.

"Oh, don't worry, sir, it's several miles out behind the reef."

"Jolly good...jolly good."

"Did you want to see me, sir?" I repeated.

"Oh never mind, mate, it wasn't important...see you tonight at dinner."

Mr. Charlesworth always had a tactful way of getting things done.

THE ENCOUNTER

The villagers had, on more than one occasion, warned me about spearfishing alone. It wasn't that I didn't appreciate their good advice; it's just that I couldn't find anyone who was interested in being in the water seven days a week, ten hours a day. Even my buddy Carlton considered this work, not play, but I could not get enough of the sea. It was like being on another planet, gliding through the clear warm waters; I felt as free as the dolphins who often joined me. Every day I searched for a new unexplored diving spot.

"Why wasn't I brought into this world as a fish?" I would wonder. "A shark...yeah, that would be fun."

If I'm ever reincarnated,
If I'm ever recreated,
I hope I come in with a big dorsal fin,
And lungs to keep me inflated.

I'd cruise up and down the shoreline,
Oh, would I have me a good time,
Scaring the wits out of adults and kids,
With this long gray body of mine.

From the Song LORD OF THE SEA

One day, I had a small boat anchored in about twenty feet of water near Crab Cay, a small island next to Green Turtle. I was spearing fish near the cliffy coast, when out of nowhere a six-foot tiger shark zipped by and snatched a grouper I had just speared. He not only got away with my fish, but also my spear.

I panicked...it was my first shark encounter in which I was the hunted. The cliffs were closer than the boat; so in an instant I was sitting on a small jagged ledge, shaking and thanking God for sparing me.

Almost an hour passed; and I was too scared to get back into the water, but I couldn't sit there forever. Trying to climb the rocky cliff wouldn't have helped since no one lived on Crab Cay to give assistance. And, if Roger or Mr. Charlesworth had to come searching...OH, NO, I didn't even want to think about it.

I had worked up enough nerve to attempt a quiet swim

for my boat, when I saw the dark figure slowly cruising by again. And who says sharks are dumb? Then he disappeared, just to make another teasing approach. If I just had had my spear, I would have felt better about a short swim to the boat. Every time I got up my nerve, my friend would reappear.

I imagined him underwater, laughing at me. Burning in the hot tropical sun, I imagined a lot of crazy things.

"Maybe he's a relative of that shark I killed a few weeks ago," I thought to myself. "Yeah, he smells the scent of his dead friend on me...he's out for revenge!" My thoughts were interrupted by the sound of a boat engine. There in the far distance, I could see a small aluminum boat. It was Lonnie, Carlton's brother, and Archie, their father.

"Hey...over here! Help!"

"OVER HERE!" I yelled, and swore to myself over the embarrassing situation.

It seemed with the hum of their engine, they couldn't hear me. Even if they had noticed my boat, it wouldn't have been an unfamiliar sight to them. They knew I spent all my time in this area. I must have supposed right, for they just kept going. As a last effort, I took off my brightly colored shorts, mooning the crabs and snails keeping me company on the rocky cliff; and I started waving my makeshift flag back and forth, screaming as loud as I could.

"HEY, ARE YOU GUYS BLIND! OVER HERE! LONNIE...ARCHIE...WAKE UP!"

It worked; they were turning around. When Archie and Lonnie saw me, all they could do was laugh.

"Ha ha ha," I said. "Very funny; just get my boat please...I'm in no mood for jokes."

While Lonnie pulled my boat to shore, Archie just gave me that "I told you so" look. In the excitement of my rescue, I had forgotten to put my shorts back on. Maybe that's what they were laughing at?

On my return to the Club, Mr. Charlesworth was pacing the dock.

"Well, mate, is everything all right?"

"Of course, sir. Why?"

"You should know by now, George, that you can't hide anything on this island. It's on every C.B. radio channel that you were attacked by a shark!"

"WHAT? ATTACKED BY A SHARK! I DON'T BE-LIEVE IT!"

Amazing! And the whole incident had only happened within the last few hours. If someone could figure out the island's rapid communications system and market it, use of the telex would be non-existent.

Later that evening, over the static crackling of the Club's C.B. radio, I listened as my story was told and retold to all the surrounding islands.

"Mavis...Mavis, come in...Mavis, this is Green Turtle."

"Mavis 'ere...go to channel nine."

Click...click.

"On channel nine."

"Mavis, did you 'ear 'bout that crazy foreigner from the Green Turtle Club?"

Crackle...crackle. (static)

"Archie and some of the boys saw 'im today naked as the day 'e born, sittin' in da boiling sun on Crab Cay."

Crack...crack. (more static)

"Those foreigners...they're all sent 'ere by Satan, you know..."

"I believe 'im go dere to smoke."

"Yeah, you right, Mavis...dat boy's a singer from America, and all of dem boys smoke ganja."

"Lord, Lord...may 'e be wit us."

Crack...crack. (even more static)

"Mavis, Mavis, this is Sybil 'ere...go to channel twelve."

Click, click.

"Going to twelve."

"You know what Joe said? If that blonde 'aired foreigner gets close to one of our children, Joe goin' to put a spear in 'im and dump 'im off Whale Cay."

Crack...crack.

"I'm going to Immigration tomorrow...this is my island...I'm 'ere to stay and 'e's 'ere to go!"

While my ears burned, I listened in fascination, switching from channel to channel. I must have heard twenty different versions of why this foreigner was sitting on the ledge of a deserted island without his pants on, but never once did anyone mention...the shark.

Oh, well, in the islands, like trade winds and sunshine, gossip is always in the air.

THE VISITORS

When the weather is right, the Gulf Stream that runs between Florida's eastern shore and the Bahamas can be as smooth as a pond. This brings out many smaller craft, who can easily make the approximately 50-mile run across for a weekend in the islands.

One fine, typical, tropical hot day, a few young cocky gentlemen were gassing up their rather expensive looking boat at Green Turtle Club's dock. Complete with two 120 horsepower outboards, impressive navigating gear, and first-class diving equipment—these guys would have awed Jacques Cousteau.

I was shooting the breeze with a few lovely lady "yachties" and couldn't help but pick up on the conversation that started between Alexander and the two fellows. They were paying for gas, and Alexander was about to give them their change.

"Keep it, dude, just have some ice ready in a few hours; we're going to the other side for some lobster," said one of the boatmen.

His partner confirmed that they would need plenty of ice to keep the lobster cool that they planned on selling in Fort Lauderdale.

"No crawfish on da ot'er side," said Alexander.

"Come on, dude, you just wanna keep them all yourself." With that they sped away in their 19-foot Mako, leaving a wake that brought curses from yachties long into the peaceful, sunny morning.

On their return late that same afternoon, Alexander had several large bags of ice ready for them; however, they had no lobster.

"Oh well, we'll get them in the morning...didn't have too much luck today," said the more talkative of the two.

"No crawfish on da ot'er side," said Alexander again, as he handed them their ice.

"Look, dude, see these large plastic bags? Tomorrow they will be full of lobster tails; at $3.60 a pound, we're gonna make ourselves rich this weekend."

"No crawfish on da ot'er side."

"Okay, dude, okay, we'll bring a few back for your dinner."

Again they filled up with gas and docked the expensive vessel for the evening.

Several afternoons later as they gassed up for the fifth time, I asked them how it had been going on the other side. Sort of frustrated, one snapped back, "Hey, man...this is the weirdest place we've ever been. There's no lobster around here. We're going back to Lauderdale. If the fish warden don't catch us, we hope to get enough to pay for this trip."

As they emptied melted ice into the sea, Alexander said

a final time, "No crawfish on da ot'er side."

This really struck a sore spot with the talkative fellow who was reaching in the bottom of his pocket in order to find enough money to pay for the fill up. "Okay, then, dude, you're so smart...we give up...where are they?"

Alexander, not saying a word, stepped into their boat, put on a face mask and jumped overboard—clothes, shoes, and all. An instant later, he popped out of the water holding a flopping lobster in each hand. He tossed the spiny creatures at their feet and re-confirmed, "NO CRAWFISH ON DA OT'ER SIDE; DEY ALL ON DIS SIDE." This brought cheers and applause from yachties tied up around the dock area. Embarrassed and broke, the two pulled away from the Green Turtle Club without saying another word. Needless to say, they were never seen again.

I had learned a long time ago it's silly to question the knowledge of the islanders when it comes to the weather, the sea, or where and when the fish are biting.

People of

the Out-Islands

III

The Caymans—
"Islands Time Forgot"

Green Turtle Cay was my home for nearly two years. During that time, I married a young (age fifteen to be exact) island girl. This, however, did not stop my wandering.

When the club closed for the off-season months (September through mid-December), I'd search out new shores: the Hawaiian Islands, for example.

In Oahu, I performed at military clubs, steamy bars, and for tourists along the Waikiki sand. Here, too, (between beachcombing) my head was buried inside travel books and atlases at any available library. This is where I discovered the Cayman Islands. Their unusual geographical location, as compared to other West Indian islands, captivated my lust for more travel.

I wrote letters to all four of Cayman's hotels, inquiring if they could use a minstrel. I received only one reply...It came from Bruce and Doris Parker, owners of the Rum Point Club.

From what I recall, their letter went something like this.....

Dear George,

We received your badly spelled note. Our hotel is small and our mosquitoes plentiful; however, if you don't mind doing extra work like bartending, raking the beach and teaching snorkeling to our guests, we'll take you on.

Can't pay you more than $40.00 per week. Have no place for you to sleep yet (we've got lots of hammocks), but we'll feed you plenty.

Sincerely,
Bruce and Doris Parker
P.S. Enclosed, our brochures.

This letter was waiting on my return to the Bahamas. Anxious to get fresh sand between my toes, I took the offer, giving it no second thought. Besides that, immigration officials on Abaco were asking more questions than usual about my long extended stays at the Green Turtle Club.

My young bride, Marsha, wasn't crazy about the idea, but there was no sense in arguing with this tropical wanderer. I was as good as gone.

I can't remember what was worse...the road to Rum Point or the mosquitoes; however, the beauty of the place soon made me forget the rear pounding trip and pesky humming creatures.

Rum Point is probably as far as you can drive from George Town, Grand Cayman, without ending up in the sea. It had a great little beach set in idyllic tropical splendor; and just a few hundred feet off the shore, coral gardens, fish and lobster were abundant.

Bruce gave me a quicky tour of the Rum Point grounds. "This is the spot," he said, pointing toward a jagged piece of iron shore, "where a ship wrecked nearly a century ago. She had just left Jamaica loaded down with barrels of rum, each barrel holding about 75 gallons. A nor'wester storm came up and tossed her over the reef. When the islanders reached here, the beach was littered with rum barrels."

"Wow, what a party they must have had," I said.

"Party! Some folks around here still have hangovers."

"Bruce, I like this place; how long can I stay?"

"Let's see how it goes...if your guitar brings in enough money to cover your salary and food expenses, you can stay till the end of May; that's when our season ends."

What added a special touch to the Rum Point Club was the main bar and restaurant. The place made you feel like you were dining in the middle of the South Pacific, on a tropical atoll.

The decor was the creation of Bruce's wife, Doris. This ex-beauty queen from New Jersey had tropics on the brain. The roof was done completely out of thatch leaves, and the windows were bordered in split bamboo, using only screening—no glass. Shells entangled in fishing lines made wind chimes, and fresh hibiscus flowers adorned every table.

Added on to the bar and restaurant facilities were a dozen flimsy rooms for rent. I can't say much about the rooms; however, the type of clientele staying at Rum Point spent little time in their rooms. The outdoors were just too gorgeous.

I spent the early part of 1971 at the Rum Point Club. During the lunch hour, boats dropped visitors from the main side of the island; and I would do my thing. "Yellow bird...up high in banana tree...De Mr. Tally man, tally me banana...daylight come and me wanna go home..." Etc...Etc...

We decided to build up the evening business with a little publicity in the local weekly paper. "APPEARING TONIGHT GEORGE NOWAK - SINGING YOUR FAVORITE ISLAND MELODIES."

"No..., we all said, 'George' won't draw people here...George is too plain, too everyday...too American sounding."

But who could I be? We needed a name to suit the South Sea flavor of Rum Point. So, many rum punches later, "The Barefoot Boy" was created...and it fit; it was me, since the nicest pair of footwear I owned were my Voit diving flippers.

A tourist was bound to be more curious to hear "The Barefoot Boy" sing a calypso than "George Nowak."

A small ad produced a large weekend crowd...mostly islanders, mixed with a few tourists. Sitting in a corner, wearing a flowered shirt, cut-off jeans and tambourine on my right foot, I sang way into the wee hours of the mosquito-filled night.

The islanders requested Hank Williams, while tourists requested "Belafonte." The Parkers bustled about mixing drinks and serving Greenie's (Heineken beer). This was one of the largest gatherings since the famous shipwreck. Doris and Bruce were delighted, and I was content as ever. I had found myself another tropical home, getting along just fine with my new hosts, who were as much in love with the islands as I was.

Bruce once held a long distance-world record for water skiing from Miami to Nassau, Bahamas. Rum Point Club was filled with his trophies and other awards proving his feats as an all around world champion skier. Doris was a professional model and scuba diving instructor before settling in Cayman. She was certainly very attractive, and by the way, an excellent cook.

The season passed quickly, and by now I had convinced my young bride to join me at Rum Point. She quickly got bored. The sun, sand, and sea held no great attraction for someone born and raised in the Bahamas; but I...I was having a blast, building thatched huts, scuba diving, and enjoying life to its limits.

I had not lost interest in the Bahamas—quite the contrary. There was, however, a future for myself in Cayman. First off, there were no immigration hassles; I was working with a legal working permit. Secondly, I was getting a little recognition singing tropical melodies.

During the early '70s, no form of regular entertainment

existed on the island. There were a few good local bands that played off and on, usually on weekends; but there was no TV or radio station, and only the occasional Kung-Fu movie was shown against the wall of some building while mosquitoes dined on the audience. So for someone who was willing to strum a guitar seven days and nights a week, I had come to the right place, at the right time.

In order for the Rum Point Club to keep its doors open during the off-season summer months, Bruce and Doris created the Rum Point Summer Camp package. They sold this idea during the winter season to guests who might be interested in getting rid of their kids for a month during school holidays. At Rum Point, the kids could enjoy something different from regular summer camps; they could learn to scuba, go deep-sea fishing and return with a great tropical tan.

The Summer Camp idea sold, so instead of heading directly back to the Bahamas, I persuaded Marsha to stay on. We were given the position of camp counselors.

The first group of all boys arrived at Rum Point just as the off-season seemed unbelievably peaceful. It took only a few hours to understand why these kids were sent away for the summer. They were all between the ages of 10 and 14, and most of them came from wealthy families...and most were spoiled BRATS!

They complained about everything..."What, hot dogs and beans again?" "How come I can't smoke? My dad lets me smoke!" "Where's the tennis court?" and so on. And when I tried to do the good-old campfire songs like "Row, row, row your boat, gently..."—I got booed! "Hey, man, don't you know any Deep Purple?" "Yeah, how about the Grateful Dead?" "Where are the topless island girls?"

Punks!!! And this was only the first group of three that we would have to contend with that summer.

Bruce had promised that the highlight of the summer camp would be the survival trip. We were to be dropped off at a remote beach on the east end of the island...a beach that had no access, except by way of a thirty-minute boat trip. We would be left there for three days and two nights with only our fishing gear, masks, snorkels, and a machete.

I must admit it sounded exciting...after all it's what I've always wanted to do. This would give me the chance to play Robinson Crusoe to the fullest.

I really didn't have time to think much about it. Before long we were waving goodbye to Bruce as he headed back toward Rum Point, leaving us stranded on the remote beach with fourteen complaining brats!

"Hey, man, how come I couldn't bring my radio?" "I'm not sleeping on this beach!" "My dad's a lawyer...he's gonna sue!"

PUNKS!

To insure we wouldn't starve, Bruce left with us, a young Caymanian by the name of Roy. Roy could easily hack open a coconut and knew just where to throw a fishing line. In case of some unexpected emergency, Roy knew the bush. He could find his way on foot to North Side Village some six rugged, densely wooded miles away. As for myself, I was going to make the best of this—brats or no brats.

After clearing a small area under a grape tree, I chopped some coconut fronds and made us a mat to sleep on. Though rain was nowhere in sight, my makeshift home would not have looked complete without a thatched roof. While I built, Marsha collected driftwood for a fire. Roy and the kids were in the sea, fishing and playing. Except for menacing sand flies, the first evening was perfect. We steamed lobster, drank coconut water, and ate fresh mangos.

Through swaying palm fronds, I watched the moon, counted stars, and enjoyed the tranquility of it all. It was all too perfect...too ideal. Tomorrow was bound to bring something bad.

Roy woke us, bright and early. "Have some breakfast, Mr. George?"

"Nah, I'll pass," figuring it would be leftover lobster and coconut water.

"How 'bout some coffee den?"

"Coffee!...Who's got coffee?"

"On de fire, sir. You wan' milk and suga'?"

"What?"

I jumped to my feet, and for a second I thought the whole isolated beach trip was a dream. Not so...there at the campfire, bacon was sizzling, eggs frying and coffee perking.

"Where did this stuff come from?" I screamed.

Roy, with a guilty look on his face, passed a cup of coffee. I wanted it badly, but refused—it was against survival rules.

One kid, stuffing his face with fresh homemade bread dripping with guava jelly and butter running through his fingers, said, "It's my fault...I'll have to take the blame."

No one else said anything. Roy started a slow guilty pace toward the beach.

"It's not Roy's fault....he did it for us...we paid him."

"Paid him! Where did you get the money?"

"We brought it with us. You said no radios, no food, no sodas. You didn't say NO MONEY!"

Roy and I discussed the whole matter under a coconut tree.

"Mr. George...dem kids got more money den Cayman have mosquitoes, and what dey pay me las' night to go to North Side, why that more money den I make me in two week time."

"But, Roy, it's supposed to be a survival trip", I protested.

"We survivin'," he said, looking a bit puzzled.

He had a good point, and I figured it would be dumb to start an argument about it; besides that, the coffee was good. If I had had second thoughts about quarreling over the situation...the six-pack of beer erased that.

Two more groups of campers followed this bunch, and each survival trip became more of a feast than the one before. Roy became more enterprising, increasing his rate for food deliveries.

What was supposed to be a test of endurance on a deserted, isolated beach turned into some of the most memorable, fun times spent during my early years in Grand Cayman.

The good Lord was being extra good to me; I couldn't understand why. Every day brought a new adventure in the sun. I was living an endless summer; I had stopped growing up. I wanted to advance no further in life than this. The future meant nothing; living day to day, there were no worries about tomorrow.

SOMEDAY I MIGHT WAKE UP,
REALIZE WHERE I AM,
DREAMIN' LIKE SOME TEN-YEAR-OLD,
OUT IN DISNEYLAND,
THERE IS NO TOMORROW,
WHEN YOU'RE LIVING IN A DREAM...

From the Song LIVING IN A DREAM

OFF TO THE GALLEON

During this fabulous time of my life, I met up with Dave Mitchell, manager of the Galleon Beach Hotel. The "Galleon," as it was known to the locals, was one of the biggest hotels on Grand Cayman at the time (40 rooms). On Friday and Saturday nights, it was the hot spot for dancing, partying, and rumming. Over a few cold beers on Rum Point's beach, Dave and I struck up a deal.

"How does $20.00 a night sound?" asked Dave.

"Great. Do I play every night?"

"No, can't afford it every night...let's play three nights a week."

"You've got yourself a Barefooted minstrel. By the way, where are you from, Dave?"

"Canada."

"Oh, so you were in the hotel business up there?"

"No...I was a fisherman, off the coast of British Columbia."

"So, how does a Canadian fisherman end up in the Caribbean as hotel manager?"

"I've got a rich uncle," he said, with a slight smirk.

"A rich uncle? What does that have to do with anything?"

"He owns the hotel."

In the early 1970s, Grand Cayman's small capital, George Town, consisted of a few banks and a couple of grocery stores. Best of all there was no Burger King, no Kentucky Fried, and no traffic jams.

Hey, don't get me wrong...not that I don't enjoy a good Whopper or a Colonel Sanders chicken leg now and then; but somehow these fast food outlets don't fit into my ideal image of an "island." The majority of Cayman's people had not yet been exposed to television, pop music, or home computers, so they lived a simple, complaisant life that revolved around men going off to sea while women cared for their children.

Few tourists knew of these Islands. If someone in Chicago mentioned they had just returned from a Grand Cayman holiday, their friends usually responded with, "Grand Canyon?"

Cruise ships did not bother to stop there. There were few shops selling souvenirs; and things were so laid back, even the taxi drivers would give an occasional complimentary island tour.

About the liveliest spot was the Galleon, located right smack on the best strip of sand on the breathtaking seven-mile beach. It was the favorite gathering spot for visitors and local residents alike. On any given weekend night, the Galleon would shake, rattle, and roll with the sound of reggae and calypso. The band was hot...the crowds were congested, and Dave was rolling in cash...until one disastrous night.

It was New Years Eve. In advance, Dave had sold some 700 dance tickets at five dollars a shot. The dance was to start at nine o'clock. By eight forty-five not one band member had shown up.

Dave was pacing the hotel lobby, and the natives were getting restless. Rum and champagne were already flowing...it was time to DANCE. Then at nine, Dave heard the sound of a trumpet.

"THANK GOD...what a relief," Dave thought. "They're here."

But THEY weren't here...only HE was here...out of a seven piece band, only the horn player had bothered to show up.

Dave, with the help of a few off-duty police officers, prevented a near riot and the possible lynching of a trumpeter by refunding everyone's money. Shortly after that, my three night a week job turned into a full time engagement. A good, hot, seven-piece band is a tough act to follow for a solo performer. However, I had one great advantage...I showed up for work.

DA MOVIE MAN

Wednesday nights were "movie nights" at the Galleon.
The films would finally make their way to Grand Cayman
after being run through every broken down projector from
Trinidad to Jamaica.

One lazy, hot, boring Wednesday afternoon, Dave came
out to the beach bar with some exciting news.

"Guess what movie we've got tonight, guys?"

"The Kung-Fu King Strikes Again!" I shouted with a sarcastic roll of my eyes.

"Godzilla meets Frankenstein," said Alberto the short,
Costa Rican bartender.

These were about the caliber of films featured on a normal movie night.

"No," said Dave, "Hold on to your hats...THE DIRTY
DOZEN!"

"THE DIRTY DOZEN!" repeated four bar patrons in sync
with each other.

"WOW, that's a great movie," someone shouted.

"Wat! Dat a good flim. Me gon bring me wife, me girlfriend
an' me children," shouted the Jamaican gardener.

"I better order some more beer...it's gonna be a big night,"
said Alberto.

The rest of the afternoon, bar patrons were in heavy
discussion over their favorite scene or favorite actor in the
film. As always, in the islands, news spread fast. By six p.m.
the crowd started pouring in: kids, grandmas, uncles, dogs
and of course, mosquitoes.

A large screened porch with more holes than screen
served as the movie house. Mosquitoes as well as patrons
found little difficulty sneaking in without paying the dollar
admission charge.

The admission take went to "The Movie Man" as he was

known...a short, unshaved, three-toothed islander, who ran the projector and distributed the films. Dave made his money at the bar. He had it set up that "The Movie Man" would take his sweet time changing reels. These intermissions allowed the audience plenty of time to swamp the bar for beer, potato chips and meat patties.

As the first reel to "The Dirty Dozen" projected into the dark, the viewers cheered and applauded with delight. This was the best motion picture shown on the island since "The Revenge of the Karate Queen," starring Chung Chee Lee.

"The Movie Man" took his usual snooze on a lounge chair as over 200 engrossed eyes watched the screen. About forty-five minutes passed, and Telly Savalas had just said, "Okay, men let's get 'em," when the reel ended. The flip-flapping of the film flopping about the projector woke "The Movie Man" and the audience gave a big, "OHHHHHH!" But they knew that after a beer break, there was more to come. Everyone rushed to the bar, and Alberto dished out the brew while Dave smiled with every ring of the register.

When the porch lights dimmed, the crowd, like a herd of elephants, rushed back to their seats. "The Movie Man," however, was still sorting out the film. He seemed to be having a problem finding the next reel. The lights went back on, and about fifteen more minutes passed.

"The Movie Man" held a piece of film to the light, put down that reel, and did the same with another, then another. Finally, he placed a reel on the projector and threaded the film.

The audience applauded wildly, the lights went out and "The Movie Man" made an announcement. "Ladies and Gentlemen...wha' you see, dat preview of a flim...soon to come...now, tonight's movie 'GODZILLA AND THE FLY.'"

Typical...typical tropical...

THE THIEF

It was such a regular occurrence that nobody gave a power failure a second thought. We would figure some drunk had hit a light pole or the utility company had run low on fuel again.

One extra hot summer morning, the heat seeped its way into my room at the Galleon. The power had been off for some five hours, and what little cool my air conditioner had put out had long gone. It was about four in the morning; and now my room had a sauna atmosphere, and I couldn't sleep. I knew Dave was an early riser, so I stumbled across the hallway and knocked on his door, hoping to bum some coffee.

"Shhh," said Dave as he greeted me at the door.

"What's up?" I whispered.

"Got some coffee on the gas stove...get a cup and QUIET-LY come out to the porch," he instructed.

The manager's suite was enormous, complete with kitchen, living room, bar, extra large bedrooms, and double bath. It sat on the top story, overlooking the property on the beach side. The large porch gave a great view of anything going on in the area.

I joined Dave on the porch.

"Down there...shh...look," he whispered.

"Hey, that's Big Bob. What's he doing?"

"Watch him and you'll see," said Dave.

"I can't believe it...he's stealing your cement blocks! Aren't you going to stop him?"

"No...just leave him."

"Leave him? But Dave..."

"Shhh...leave him."

The hotel was in the process of building a new beach barbecue area, so Dave had ordered some 250 cement blocks to get the project started. These blocks were stacked up along the hotel's wall.

Big Bob worked as a dive instructor for the water sports center operating out of the hotel. In the moonlight, you could see Bob's pickup parked in the bushes about two hundred yards from the cement blocks. Two blocks at a time, one in each hand, Big Bob labored back and forth through sandspurs, shrubs, and bushes. His panting could be heard above the gentle lapping of the waves. In Cayman, during the month of July, with no wind, even the early hours of morning can be uncomfortably hot.

We watched for over an hour, amazed at this guy's gall. Here he was in broad moonlight, helping himself to the hotel's property. Bob took an occasional rest to look at his blistered hands and wipe sweat from his forehead. Dave said nothing.

"Dave, you can't let him get away with this!"

"Shhhhhhhhhh, quiet," said Dave chuckling lightly.

"Talk about pirates; it's rumored this guy is building himself a house."

"Yeah, with my cement blocks," whispered Dave.

As the sunlight made its slow entrance into the quiet morning, Big Bob's truck was filled to capacity. Even the front seat had cement blocks stacked on it.

"They must weigh twenty pounds apiece," I said in amazement. "There's no way he'll move that truck in this soft sand."

"You know something," said Dave. "I think you're right; he'll never move that truck."

Dave broke the morning silence, "HEY, BOB...You'll never move that truck in this soft sand...SO YOU MIGHT AS WELL PUT EVERY SINGLE BLOCK BACK...NOW!!!"

Poor Big Bob. What could he do...What could he say? He was caught red-handed. Two blocks at a time, one in each blistered hand...he labored till near lunch time, returning every single block. Dave's revenge was just the pure enjoyment of watching the modern-day pirate struggle and toil in the sweltering heat.

YELLOW BIRD

Now, there's no question about it, the number one song on the Tourist Hit Parade is and always has been, "Yellow Bird." If I had collected a dollar for every time I've sung this island classic, I could buy my own island. No Caribbean holiday is complete without a good tan, a rum punch, and a dance under the stars to the tune of YELLOW BIRD.

Now as far as most local residents are concerned, they would like to take that YELLOW BIRD and shoot him off his banana tree. It's the last song they want to hear. However, this minstrel knows where his bread and butter is coming from. So, I gladly play Yellow Bird any time our valued tourists want to hear it.

If there is anyone who hates the tune more than my close friend Reid Dennis, I haven't met him yet. Reid, an ex-Marine Captain, is as red-necked, all-American as they come. Give him a keg of beer and an Earl Scruggs banjo special and he's in heaven.

One evening I was about to start my first set with a full house of rum punch drinking, sunburned tourists when Reid called me over to the bar.

"Barefoot, please don't play that damn Yellow Bird tonight...how about a little George Jones or Merle Haggard?"

"Reid ol' pal...we've been through this a thousand times; I'm not here to please you...see those people out there...that's where I make my living."

Just when I thought I'd made my point, the bartender butts in, "Yeah, Foot, why do you play that song ten times every night?"

"Why do you make pina coladas every night?" I snapped back. With that I walked on stage, opening my set with YELLOW BIRD, which I dedicated to Reid and the bartender.

Several whiskeys later, Reid was in the mood for revenge. With me totally unsuspecting, he put together one of the best organized tricks to be played on any performer.

I was in the middle of set number two, when a bony-legged tourist handed me a note:

WE JUST ARRIVED. COULD YOU PLEASE PLAY YELLOW BIRD FOR ELMA AND FRED? IT'S OUR 20TH WEDDING ANNIVER-SARY...THANKS, FRED.

Folded up in the note was a crisp ten dollar bill.

"Ladies and gentlemen I have a re-run request; this is going out to Elma and Fred tonight, on their 20th wedding anniversary. Elma, Fred, this is for you."

I strummed a few soft chords and started singing, "YELLOW BIRD UP, HIGH IN BANA..."

With that, every single person including bartenders, waitresses, beach bums, and Reid, got up and walked out.

Over 200 people marched out, one right after the other. It reminded me of a fire drill back in my school days. The nightclub was empty before I got into the second verse. What could I do?????????

I just kept on singing; and when the song was over, they all filed back in. In a nightclub filled with laughter, Reid shouted, "Hey, Barefoot, NOW can I hear some Merle Haggard?"

I know when I'm defeated. I began a thirty-minute medley of Haggard's greatest hits.

abebooks.com

$8⁰⁰

Signed by author

IV

"Nassau—It's Not Always Better In The Bahamas"

If you took time to read the preface in this book, you'll recall that I warned you this would be a potpourri of stories. This story, about my unexpected visit to Nassau (capital of the Bahamas) has been my biggest headache in the writing of this book.

My publisher, Dennis Bartow, warned me the expense of any last minute changes would come out of my royalties. Well, there have been lots of last minute changes in this particular narrative. I've had continuous debates with myself about whether this gloomy part of my life would fit into a book about endless happy tropical summers.

Let's be realistic. Even beachcombers have their ups and downs. Alexander Selkirk, who inspired the story of Robinson Crusoe, was booted off ship after quarreling with his captain. Until he took control of the solitude he was then faced with, his island was for him the greatest of horrors.

Most beachcombers are true strangers in paradise. They wander about in the balmiest weather with a constant cloud of suspicion hanging over them.

Who is he?

Where did he come from?

I've seen his photo in the post office.

I hear he's dodging the draft

...and so on.

For the people who know me, here's my side of a story that has been fabricated, twisted, and idle-talked in so many versions. And for the reader who doesn't know me—the person who bought this book because of that magic word on the cover "ISLANDS"—this is to prove that you can be skipping down a sandy beach, chased by beautiful naked island girls, caressing a bottle of rum, the sun bronzing your skin, a fresh floral scented breeze flowing through your hair, when all of a sudden you trip on a conch shell...AND BREAK YOUR NECK. Some island residents have a more blunt description of this...

"IT'S JUST ANOTHER SHI... DAY IN PARADISE."

Those scenes on the silver screen have always amazed me...there's a barroom brawl, and the first thing the musicians do is smash their $800 guitars over someone's head... or put some drunk through a $500 bass drum.

I guess if some Hollywood producer is picking up the tab, that's all fun and games; but in real life, most musicians are making monthly payments on their cherished instruments, and most musicians are lovers...not fighters. Yours truly definitely falls in the "lover" category.

However, one December while playing music for the Green Turtle Club's Christmas party, I managed to get involved in a bit of a brawl. After trying every possible angle to get out of the situation, and dodging a few well-aimed punches targeted toward me, I delivered a reluctant blow. The incident put a damper on the happy mood of the evening, and everyone quickly departed.

The next day, Christmas eve, I was on a small Air Bahamas prop jet to the capital, Nassau. Sitting beside me was Sergeant Detective Rollings of the Bahamian C.I.D. squad (Criminal Investigation Department). He pulled a pad from his briefcase and started taking notes.

"Now, Mr. Nowak, tell me again exactly what 'appened

and the truth please."

"I've got nothing to hide. Can't you take these handcuffs off? Where am I going on this little plane?"

"Regulations," he answered.

I went through my story for the tenth time, and then he asked for a rerun. As we started our descent into Nassau, I said, "Look, we should have this cleared up by this evening. What's the possibility of my going back to Abaco on the late flight?"

"Mr. Nowak, maybe you don't realize the mess you're in...by this evening you could be charged with murder."

By that evening, to my disbelief, I was charged. The unfortunate man whom I took a swing at went into a coma and stayed there until he passed away that same day. I repeat...I'm no fighter, nor am I easily provoked. It was one of those one in a million jabs, then the poor fellow landed in the wrong place (the corner of a table) at the wrong time (when I was there).

At Fox Hill Prison, the Bahamian Government's central penitentiary, I paced my small cell as broadcasted Christmas music echoed through the corridors.

This doesn't make any sense at all, I thought. *What did I do? I just defended myself. I can't be charged with MURDER!*

A few days later, I was again telling my story, this time to an old graying attorney sent by my in-laws. His unpressed suit looked to be several sizes too big, and his briefcase consisted of a large manila envelope stuffed with papers.

"I normally don't work during the 'olidays, but your father-in-law is a good friend, so 'ere I am," he said.

"When can I get out of here? I can't take this...did anyone tell the authorities my wife is about to have a baby?" (Marsha was 8 1/2 months pregnant.)

"George, this is a serious charge...wife or no wife, you are going to be 'eld until the P.I."

"P.I.? What's that?"

"Preliminary Inquiry—to see if there is any evidence to 'old you over for trial."

"For trial? Why? I didn't do anything except defend myself; that guy wanted to punch my lights out!"

"Sorry, George. The Commissioner on Green Turtle Cay will decide that."

Later that evening, my dinner of peas and rice, corned beef, and Bahamian bread was getting cold. I had no appetite; I was at the lowest point of my beach roving days. I'd always wanted to visit Nassau...but certainly NOT LIKE THIS. Though I had never taken my good life or freedom for granted, I had never appreciated so much what, at that moment, I didn't have.

In the corner of my cell, where the brick wall joined the metal bars, a hand appeared. "Merry Christmas, neighbor; my name's Allen." I could tell from the firm handshake and the southern drawl, my neighbor was not a Bahamian.

"Yeah, yeah, same to you. I'm George."

"What they got you for, George?"

I couldn't see Allen for the wall between us, but I felt embarrassed to tell him of my charge.

"Hey, George, you still there?"

"Yeah, they say I'm charged with murder."

"MURDER? Wow. That's tough, man. They still hang people in these islands for that."

"Gee, thanks, pal. That's all I need this holiday season."

"Sorry. You got any cigarettes?"

"No, I don't smoke."

"Let me give you some good advice, George. Get some cigarettes—they're like money here. You're only being held for trial, so you can have all the cigarettes you want. Have your family bring them."

I learned from our conversation that sentenced prisoners like Allen were allowed only a limited amount of cigarettes, so a pack of nicotine would buy you a hot cup of coffee instead of diluted cold brown water, or a fish fillet instead of a fish head. I had my in-laws bring several cartons of the tobacco-currency. Allen's advice was certainly helpful. Not only did I eat well (once my appetite returned), but I also had clean blankets and pillowcases daily.

It was January the 11th, and still no date had been set for my inquiry. I had been in Fox Hill Prison for over two weeks. Despite my large portions of food and interesting conversations with Allen, I was feeling more depressed than ever.

"Hey, cheer up, man. There's nothing you can do but wait. I had to wait three months before my P.I. came up," Allen warned.

"Oh, don't tell me that...I can't live that long without sun and ocean."

"You got a Bahamian family backing you. You won't have to wait too long. Anyway, they caught me with a plane full of drugs on San Salvador Island. I also shot a Bahamian Customs agent in the foot. I'll be here forever. Twenty-two years was my sentence. In this hell-hole, that's forever."

"Allen, there's a big difference between shooting someone in the foot and being charged with murder," I replied.

"You got a point, but don't forget, I shot a Bahamian, a local citizen. In your case, it was a foreigner. That will make a big difference."

I was trying to find some reassurance in his words when a guard opened my cell.

"Best make straight your shirt, and neaten up your hair a bit," ordered the ·guard.

"What's up? Where are we going?"

"De wa'den want see you."

"The warden? Should I take my things?" I said, hoping this would be my release.

"No, you comin' back."

We walked through what seemed an endless maze of corridors, stairs and yard passages. Finally, we stopped by a large wooden door. The guard knocked.

"Enter," said a distant voice.

"Sir, this is Nowak," the guard said, standing at attention.

"Thank you, corporal. Wait outside, please," the warden ordered.

I was shaking in my flip flops as the big, neatly dressed black man handed me the receiver to his desk phone.

"'ere, it for you."

It was my mother-in-law with the first piece of good news since my arrest. I was a father. Marsha had given birth to a girl. Mother and baby were doing fine.

I handed the phone back, and the warden congratulated me, then called for the guard.

Back in my cell, I stared at the concrete ceiling. "This is all too much," I thought. "I don't know if I can handle this...a murder charge, my precious freedom lost, and now, on top of all that...fatherhood."

Only one other good thing happened during my stay in Fox Hill. I got my hands on a book called, "An Island To Oneself," by Tom Neale. The book cost a whole carton of cigarettes, but a case would have been worth it.

Reading of Tom's adventures living alone on Suwarrow Atoll in the Northern Cook Islands helped me stay halfway sane. I must have read the pages and looked at the photos a thousand times, and I was never bored. The book was an escape to what had been taken away from me. I promised myself if ever I got out of this mess, I would visit Suwarrow Atoll, come hell or high water.

January 18th, I was on a flight back to Abaco. Again,

seated next to me was Detective Rollings, and across the aisle was my baggy-suited attorney. The inquiry was set for one p.m. that afternoon on Green Turtle Cay.

As the ferry neared the dock, I had a flashback—memories of my first arrival at Green Turtle. Though the present circumstances were much different, the charm of the village always impressed me. The village dock was crowded with curious, finger-pointing locals. Most were dressed in their Sunday best. After all, this was the biggest event since the last hurricane.

As we walked to the small wooden building that served as a courthouse, the crowd followed close behind and the air was thick with gossip. I tried to look at the bright side—there's only one thing worse than being talked about and that's not being talked about.

The inquiry should have been quick and simple. Detective Rollings didn't have much to say. Neither did my aging attorney. However, everything said had to be handwritten by the local Commissioner. There was no secretary, no stenographer, no tape recorder. The torture of sitting through this inquiry was worse than any life sentence.

Detective Rollings: "I found no weapons on the premises nor did..."

Commissioner: "Wait a second, detective...you said...'I found no..' what on the premises?"

Detective Rollings: "No weapons, sir."

Commissioner: "Weapons. W-E-A-P-O-N-S, Weapons, there you go. Please continue, detective."

My Attorney: "Excuse me, sir, are you sure that's the proper spelling for weapons?"

Detective Rollings: "No, I think it's W-A-P-O-N-S..."

Commissioner: "Hold on a second, gentlemen, I've got to get a new pen. I'll be right back."

This went on and on till near sunset. Five ink pens later,

even I, the center of attention, the guy who was steps away from the gallows, found it hard to stay awake. Then the Commissioner asked Detective Rollings, my attorney and me to approach the bench.

"Gentlemen," the Commissioner said, "I see no reason to hold this man any further. This is a clear-cut case of self-defense. I've heard no evidence to carry-over to trial. Detective Rollings, I order you to release the prisoner."

And that was it...no pounding the gavel, no cheers from the spectators, no T.V. or newspaper reporters swarming about for a story. It was done, over, finito...

Thirty minutes later, I had my first glimpse of my new daughter. A week later, I was back in the Cayman Islands.

When the locals start questioning,
What he's doing or where he's been,
He just pulls up anchor and sails beyond the reef.

From the Song TROPICAL BEACHCOMBER

V

Jamaica...No Problem
or..Irie Dread..

Around 1974 or so, I advanced from being a solo act to being a trio. My little combo consisted of a young, very shy, frown-faced Caymanian guitarist named Philip "SMILEY" Bodden and a Jamaican bass player, Bertrum "Harry" Johnson.

At the time of this writing, Harry is still a member of my band and also pleases tourists several nights a week with his limbo-fire dancing. Harry is a first-class musician (most of the time) when he's not trying to get the attention of some big lady. "De bigga da betta," says Harry.

Harry is also the MASTER-OF-EXCUSES. I'll give you an example. One evening Harry made more than his usual number of musical blunders. A fast scan of the crowd showed me the root of the problem. Directly in front of the stage there sat this huge person, looking something like a Sumo-wrestler wearing a blonde wig. The more she winked at Harry, the more his bass playing resulted in sour notes. When we took our intermission, I asked Harry to see me outside.

"Harry, what's your problem?"

"No problem, Jawg (George). Wa I do, wa I do?"

"Harry, you're not paying attention...you're making too many mistakes!"

"Wa you mean mistake; wa you mean I no paying

attention?" he asked looking puzzled.

"Harry, Harry, it's like...it's like..." I was stumbling through words trying to find an example, another way to say "you're not paying attention."

Harry, still looking confused, says, "Wa, wa, wa you try say, Jawg?"

"Harry, if you pulled out of this parking lot tonight and made a left, you'd go towards West Bay...If you took a right you'd go towards George Town, RIGHT?"

"Dat Right," he answers, checking my directions. "But, Harry, if you were NOT PAYING ATTENTION you would go straight and run right into a coconut tree, maybe even kill yourself."

I felt proud about making such a good clear example. "You get my point now, Harry?"

With a look as serious as a nun in prayer, he said, "But, Jawg, me steering could be broke!"

With that he walked away, and I sort of just stood in the parking lot, trying to figure out if there was anything to be learned from Harry's theory.

It was on Harry's suggestion I went to Jamaica to record my first 45 rpm record. By the way, the number one rule in our band since that trip is...DO NOT LISTEN TO HARRY!!!

We landed in Jamaica a bit late. After a fast check through Immigration and Customs, the three of us were jammed into the back seat of a taxi. It speeded through the garbage strewn streets of Kingston, nearly demolishing a few goats.

Paying no mind to humans crossing the streets, the cabby turned around and asked, "You gwine need some spliff masa?"

"Spliff...masa? What's that he say?" I asked Harry.

"Ganja, 'im wan know if you wan ganja," explained Harry.

"Oh, you mean grass."

"Irie, irie...Dat it. Dat spliff," said the cabby.

"No thanks; the strongest thing I like from Jamaica is Red Stripe (Jamaican Beer)."

"Awrite, you wan beer den?"

"No, I don't wan beer den, I wan go to de studio or I be late," I ordered, trying sarcastically to copy his accent. With that he pressed the gas pedal, increasing his speed, past the shanties of Kingston.

We were dropped off in an industrial area on the outskirts of town.

"Is this it, Harry?" I asked.

"I tink so."

"You tink so...you tink so! You told me you used to record here, and now you 'tink' so?"

"I tink so," he reconfirmed.

Behind the high metal fence I noticed a security guard reading an Archie comic book. "Sir, excuse me...is this Reggae-Jam Recording Studio?" I asked.

"Las' time me look," he answered.

"Well, we're supposed to have started recording an hour ago; could you please let us in?"

"No wan 'ere today, sa...dey close up."

"There must be some mistake; I spoke with the engineer yesterday, and everything was all set."

Through the whole conversation, he never once took his eyes off the comic book. By now, the cruel intensity of the sun and the couldn't-care-less attitude of the security guard was testing my patience.

"Harry, would you speak some voodoo to this guy?"

Harry pressed his face against the chained steel gate and started talking with no more enthusiasm than our comic book-reading friend. "A bredda, me 'ate badda you. Leggo dat book. Da sun hot wid fiah, mek us do a ting. Im hab plenty money; I man get u ten dolla."

Harry must have hit the right note, because the guard got up from his chair (still reading) and picked up a phone.

"What did you say to him, Harry?"

"I tell 'im you plenty rich; you give 'im a few dolla' if him call engineer."

"Thanks, Harry...it's coming out of your paycheck."

Another half hour passed, and every few minutes or so a car would pull up with a few shady-looking characters.

"You wan spliff, mon?"

"No, thanks," I'd say.

"Tour de island, maybe?"

"No, thanks."

I paced the area, while Harry and Smiley practiced their harmonies under a fruitless mango tree. Finally a small foreign looking car pulled up.

"Hello...I'm Tom Goodings...your engineer."

"Correct me if I'm wrong," I said, "but weren't we supposed to start several hours ago?"

"Well, when I heard you guys were coming from Cayman, I figured for sure you were going to be late—the flight from Cayman is always late."

All I could say was, "Oh."

The studio looked as disastrous as the streets of Kingston. Tom flicked on the lights, mended a few exposed wires, and said, "Okay, I'm ready."

"Where are the musicians?" I asked.

"You booked musicians?" he responded with a surprised look on his face.

"Yes, a keyboard man and a drummer."

Tom picked up the phone. "Nigel, wha 'appened mon...dis fellow 'ere waitin' on you." That's all he said, then he hung up.

"He's coming. Don't worry, he lives just around the cor-ner, and he's bringing the drummer along with him," confirmed the engineer.

I started to relax a bit, though we were already hours late starting.

"Tom, you don't look West Indian; where you from?"

"Australia originally, but I've been engineering here for the last fifteen years."

"How do you handle this inefficiency?" I asked.

"How long have you lived in the islands?" he asked.

I got the point...so I shut my mouth and tuned my guitar. The piano player and drummer finally showed up.

"Hello, I'm George...this is Harry, and the guitarist there in the corner is Smiley."

I got a customary weak, limp West Indian handshake. Harry and Smiley received a clenched raised first and a "cool, cool, brudda."

We ran through the songs a few times. They made up for their lateness by quickly catching on to the music. I did have to calm Harry down a bit. He was playing twenty notes in the same line where we had rehearsed three. This was, of course, to impress his Jamaican bruddas. After this slight problem was cleared up, we were ready to record. However, now it was time for a short spliff break.

"Wan spliff, mon?" asked the drummer.

"No thanks; let's record!"

Ignoring me, the two hired musicians lit up a joint capable of choking a donkey.

I rushed into the control room. "Tom," I said, "look, I don't want to get in any trouble...you think you could speak with those guys about their smoking ganja in the studio?"

"Relax, relax. Jamaica is as famous for its ganja as it is for its music. These two guys don't work without it...so just relax; they'll do a good job for you."

He was right; when the red recording light went on, they never missed a note. Their timing was perfect, and the rhythm they created was contagious. One take, and I had a good, clean, unflawed recording.

It all ended too fast. I don't know if the thick smoke from their giant stogies was affecting me; but I wanted to play more, and eating up expensive studio time never entered my mind.

I had been told (by phone conversation) before arriving that each musician would cost twenty Jamaican dollars per song. I counted out their money on top of the studio piano. They watched every move of my fingers through their dark shades.

"There you go, gentlemen...that should be right...two songs, twenty dollars per song...that's eighty dollars for the both of you." With a slight grin, I said, "Thank you, that was great music." I got no response...no smile, no nod, no nothing. Something was wrong!! I picked up the money and counted again. "Ten, twenty, thirty and fifty makes eighty."

"I need ten dolla for me brudda," said the drummer.

"Ten dollars for your brother...what for; what does he have to do with this?"

"Dem his drumstick...he rent me dem."

Inside, I was about to explode. I wanted nothing more than to stuff his spliff down his throat and tell him what to do with his "brudda's" drumsticks.

But, I kept my cool. I paid up, mixed my songs and swore never to come back to this rip-off studio again. As we waited for our taxi, Harry said, "Jawg, me need ten dolla."

"Oh no, not you too, Harry!"

I was about to grab him around the neck when he explained, "No, for de guard...him been waiting."

Never say never. I did come back to Jamaica, just like the television commercial says. This time skipping Kingston and the Reggae-Jam Studios I had several pleasant stays on the island's beautiful lush north coast. Jamaica, the land

of reggae, rum and ganja is certainly worth a visit. It's hard
to find a more scenically beautiful island in all the West
Indies.

Listen Rasta Man,
I don't understand,
When you talkin' roots,
Or the Babylon,
But I admit,
I like the beat.

From the Song LIKE THE REGGAE BEAT

VI

"Fantasy Island"

By the time an average tourist has made his or her way to a nightclub, he is half full of rum, sunburned, and ready to dance out of step to a rhythmic calypso. This is fortunate for us entertainers working in the tropics. It's easy to please an audience whose sole purpose is fun, sun and rum. Now, most people in this tropical state of mind are not themselves. After all, why should they be—they're in another country, a place to hide, a place to live out fantasies, a place where they need not worry what the neighbors think or say.

One evening a very properly dressed, well-to-do looking elderly man walked up to the bandstand with a young giggling island girl by his side. While he talked, she moved about in his arms like a cobra.

"When you take your next break, I'd like to have a word with you," he said.

"Sure, sir," I responded, counting the band into the next number.

During my intermission, I found him in a dark corner enveloped in native passion while refilling crystal with expensive champagne.

"Excuse me, sir. Did you want to see me?"

"Oh yes, I've got a deal for you," he said, trying to break an octopus-like hold the young girl had on him.

"My wife and I are having our 25th anniversary next

month; could you fly up to the States and play for us?"

I gave him a fast run down on possible expenses. He passed me a business card and said, "No problem; just drop all that information in the mail, and I'll get back to you. Oh and by the way...you never saw her," pointing toward his infatuation.

Well, I thought to myself, most of these deals made during intermissions never become reality; so I wasn't too worried about not saying anything to anybody, whomever or wherever they might be.

A few evenings later, the same fellow and the same young brown-skinned gal were nose to nose as he tried carrying on a phone conversation in the hotel lobby.

"Honey...Honey, I can barely hear you," he shouted into the receiver. "Oh, the weather down here is awful; I would have been home a few days ago but my flight was canceled. Of course I miss you," he said, while one hand glided over the girl's slender, slithering body. "Okay, Honey, bye now; this hurricane should clear in a few days so I'll see you then...yes, I love you, too." As he hung up the receiver, he shouted across the hotel lobby, "Don't forget, you're coming up to play for my anniversary; still got my card?"

"Yes, sir," I responded.

He took off his shoes, rolled up his pants and like a young teenager, strutted rejuvenated into a clear, calm, star-filled tropical night, hand in hand with paradise.

What a time he's havin', I thought to myself. Somehow I sensed this would be the last I'd hear from him...I was wrong. About a month later, I found myself at a rather ritzy country club in upstate New York.

The intermission-deal came through. We were playing for a silver anniversary. It was a one-night gig, all expenses paid—with a lot of yankee dollars to boot. All went well; and after a fun evening, my island-loving friend asked,

"Could you make a hotel reservation for me on your return to Grand Cayman?"

"Gladly, sir."

He looked over his shoulder, "And if you see um, you know..."

"Yes, I know," I interrupted.

"Give her my regards and let her know when I'm coming back. Oh, and this is for your troubles."

He slipped a hundred dollar bill into my hand. At that point, I wondered if I should have mentioned that I did see her...almost every night...on the same barstool, scanning the smoke-filled nightclub for new prey.

Our conversation was broken into by a diamond-and-fur adorned lady.

"Dahling, let's go...the driver's waiting."

"Yes, dear, I'm ready," he responded, doing a Jekyll and Hyde transformation. He shook my hand, and as a reminder about his reservation, said, "I sure hope the weather is better the next time I'm down your way on business."

He never returned for his confirmed dates, and his brown-skinned, part-time companion did not remember him when I passed on his message.

Almost a year later, I received a call requesting another special one night performance. This time, I was off to Fantasy Island.

"Fantasy Island? You mean like on TV Fantasy Island?" I shouted into the receiver.

"That's close enough; are you interested in doing the job?" said the distant voice.

"How do we get there? I'm not going to my travel agent to book a trip to Fantasy Island."

"Don't worry about transportation; I'll mail you a contract and enclose all your travel information, plus a deposit."

"Well...Okay, I guess; sounds good. How did you hear

about me?"

"I've never heard you perform, but your band was recommended by a fellow in upstate New York...Do you remember that job?"

"Yes...of course."

"Well, he sends his regards and asks if the weather has cleared up in the islands yet...you're supposed to know what that means."

"I do, yes, I do."

"Anyway, see you on Fantasy Island." The long distance voice hung up.

Within a week's time, I received a registered letter. Enclosed was a hefty deposit check from Air-Jet Electronics International and a short note instructing us to be at Grand Cayman's airport on a given date and time.

The whole thing was rather mysterious...a check? A note? Fantasy Island??? What was I getting myself into???

A nine-seater Lear-jet landed at 8:45 a.m. that designated morning. The pilot and the long-distance party-coordinator introduced themselves. After a few minutes of aviation talk with the local customs people, we were shooting off to Fantasy Island.

I felt like a real star at this point. "Hey, Harry, is this the life or is this the life?"

Harry just sort of shrugged his shoulders, not wanting to show his excitement, or maybe he was just scared out of his wits as we bulleted over Cuba.

"Okay, what's up?" I asked the gayish-acting stranger serving us drinks.

"What's up? We're off to Fantasy Island...that's what's up."

"Look, my friend, this isn't Harry you're talking to. I know there's no such a place...this Lear-jet, the drinks, the money, it's all fabulous...but what's up?"

The assistant informed us we were on our way to a private

island belonging to the owners of Air-Jet Electronics International. The geographical location of the island was a secret and of no importance since the theme of this year's annual executive party was "Fantasy Island."

Guests at the party would be presidents and vice-presidents of some of the largest corporations in North America...along with a mixture of wives, lovers and secretaries.

Our job...just sing those island melodies; and Harry was to do his limbo show.

I believe Harry and Philip figured we were off to Hollywood, but I'd been to the Bahamas too often not to recognize the turquoise waters and sandy cays below. I calculated we were somewhere in the Bahamian Exuma islands as the jet taxied alongside a dozen or so other streamlined Lears. It was a beautiful little island, approximately two miles long by a quarter mile wide. Coconut trees sprouted everywhere on the well-kept grounds. There was a main house with restaurant facilities and a dock harboring miniature Queen Marys. The island was complete with skeet shoot, golf course, and several mansions.

We were all checked into private cottages along a spectacular beach. Golf carts were also provided for transportation around the island. Harry and Philip decided to check out their musical instruments and the food. I went beachcombing.

On the south end of the island, I found a long stretch of beach. I swam alone in the shallow, clear water as rays jetted through the sand. "What a spot."...I thought of Tom Neale... "Is this what it was like on Suwarrow atoll...living alone in some forgotten corner of the world?"

As I lay in a tidal pool, staring at a sky bluer than any dream I had ever imagined, the occasional puff of white clouds would cast a shadow over my relaxed body. Why,

I wondered, were these people with so much wealth transplanting their urban toys onto this paradise. Skeet shoots, golf courses, golf carts, and Lear-jets...Couldn't they leave all that in New York?

And if that isn't enough...mansions. What's wrong with a thatched hut and outrigger canoes instead of those million dollar floating apartments?

My feelings were a bit hypocritical, for I had enjoyed the jet ride and was certainly looking forward to banking away the easy cash made on this engagement.

Had I been shipwrecked here and had this been my private island, I'd have asked for no more than the brilliant hot sun on the sea and the delicious freshness of a slight breeze cooling the warm tropical air. Golf course or no golf course, I was not about to let any negative feelings get in the way of this island experience.

"Jawg, look 'ere, Jawg," shouted guess who from the beach.

"Harry, c'mon in. The water's fine."

"Wha? Not me; da watta too cold."

"Cold? Are you nuts? This is fabulous." I dove, chasing a school of multi-colored fish.

"Jawg, plenty problem; you must come."

I chuckled to myself, as I noticed Harry brushing the powdery white sand off his polished, raised shoes. Now what possibly could be a problem on this little Garden of Eden...unless Harry crashed a golf cart into a coconut tree. In slow motion, I swam to shore.

"What's the problem, Harry," I said, dripping saltwater and pleasure.

"Jawg, me can't do me limbo show tonight."

"What...why?"

"Dey 'ave no dance floor."

"Dey 'ave no dance floor?"

"No, Jawg, no dance floor."

"Harry, only you could screw up a perfect day in paradise. Let's go check it out."

Back at the main building, preparations were in full swing for the lavish party. Flowers had been flown in from New York...which was rather strange since wild hibiscus and periwinkles of every color grew on the island. Long strands of feathers were stuck into styrofoam bird forms to add a jungle effect to the decor.

Islanders were in no rush setting tables of china, sterling silver, and crystal, while European chefs prepared an endless banquet of exotic foods.

Harry and I walked to the outdoor stage area being decorated with palm fronds and fish net. As we stood on a flat cement floor directly in front of the stage, I asked, "What's wrong with this, Harry? This is obviously the dance floor."

He looked down puzzled and replied, "But, Jawg, dis is too rough; it gonna scratch my knees."

Frustrated, I got on my knees, dragging myself around like some crippled dog.

"See, Harry, it's no big deal."

"Mon...I dun' know, Jawg; dis not wat I use to."

"It's not what you're used to...NOT WHAT YOU'RE USED TO...Look, Harry, I don't understand you sometimes...here we are, all expenses paid...a ride in a private jet...two weeks salary for one night's work and you're complaining...what's your problem?"

"But, Jawg..."

"Don't but me, Harry. There are plenty of unemployed limbo dancers who would be happy and very appreciative to be in your platform shoes right now."

With that I walked away, confused at his silly protest, while Harry looked confused at his expensive shoes. I went back to the beach and swam away the minor problem. We were not the only line-up of entertainment for the evening. Look-alikes of Mr. Rourke and Tatoo were on hand to greet everyone attending the bash. The Tatoo-clone got on everyone's nerves with his constant, "It's da plane, boss, da plane." A four piece group had been brought in from Hawaii to sing during cocktail time; and when our show was over, a Glenn Miller-type orchestra took over. What a party! What money...the tropical air reeked of wealth.

The gathering was obviously a contest to see who wore the most diamonds and whose dress could outglitter them all.

Except for a few runs in the leotards Harry wears for his limbo show, all went well. No bruises, scratches, or blood. But of course, Harry had to get in the last word. "You see wat I tell you, Jawg,...look, me uniform spoiled."

A few days later, thousands of feet in the air, we were on our way back home. I was in absolute glory, thinking how lucky I was... sipping a margarita on a private jet with my pockets full of easy money. I leaned back, sank into my seat and closed my eyes.

"Hey, you guys, what do you think? What a life?"

"Jawg, you know sometin'...dem people back on dat island...dey try take advantage of us."

I blocked Harry and his bewildering remark out of my mind, then went into a deep, gratified sleep.

I'm island dreamin'
Island dreamin'
Dreamin' about the sun, sand and sea
I'm island dreamin'
Island dreamin'
Dreamin' about an island fantasy.

From the Song ISLAND DREAMING

VII

"Back To The Cayman Islands"

"THERE'S TREASURE ON THOSE BEACHES..."

In the mid-1970's, the islands time forgot (The Caymans), went through some interesting changes. They became established as a financial offshore tax-free bank haven. Sort of a tropical Switzerland. Since I've never had to pay taxes, all this meant nothing to me. However, it put Cayman on the map with bankers, millionaires, and IRS dodgers. The money-minded visitors soon spread the word, and it was no time before the peaceful, quiet shores of the seven-mile beach began mushrooming condos. If you took a short hop off the island, you'd come back a few days later to find new acres of beach property stripped of seagrape trees and replaced with cement blocks, steel and lumber.

Now, for this beachcomber, it was a sad sight the first time I spotted bulldozers noisily plowing through white sand, as coconut trees and Australian pines fell like pick-up sticks around them.

"What's going on?" I asked the operator of a big yellow machine.

"Dey gone build a big 'otel 'ere, mon."

"A BIG HOTEL. OH, NO!"

"Oh, yes. It gonna be one dem 'oliday Inn places; dey nice

you know. I stay in one at Busch Garden one time."

"A Holiday Inn...A HOLIDAY INN...THAT'S IT; IT'S THE END...A HOLIDAY INN....OHHHHHHHHH NOOOOOOO."

The native machine operator couldn't understand my disappointment, and I couldn't understand his enthusiasm to have a Holiday Inn on this tropical island.

Well, as the saying goes..."No 'man' is an island," but why can't an island be an island? I had no right to feel so selfish. After all, it wasn't my island. Immigration had reminded me about that more than once. And progress can't be restrained in a country where its people are eager for television, fast cars, and the latest fashions.

It was bound to happen; these beautiful white powdery beaches, fantastic colorful reefs, and charming people 480 miles from America could not stay lost in time forever. Then again, on a positive note, to have condos, hotels, and taxis is sure better than oil refineries or factories spoiling one's tropical vision. So, like it or not, I progressed with the progress.

Just as my urge to roam hit me again, the trade winds shifted... and so did my life. I had been separated from my Bahamian wife for nearly a year and was living a wild, crazy, sleepless, female-chasing life, talking to my reflection in the mirror each morning...

"Boy, were you dumb. Why did you ever get married? Look at the fun you're having as a bachelor. You were meant to wander, raise hell, and consume rum. Oh my, that evil demon rum. I need some Excedrin...my head feels like a piece of brain coral that's had a two ton anchor dropped on it..."

One day on the beach, under a midday sun, I found myself a treasure. Just like in a fairy tale, this Robinson Crusoe found his Girl Friday. It wasn't supposed to happen; it should have been just another typical tropical day.

Geri, a guest on board a cruise liner, had a total of eight hours to spend on these shores. I was playing music on the beach for the ship passengers. Had she decided to take the optional island tour, we would have never met that day.

Through a mob of some 800 sun-seeking tourists, we made eye contact. Yes, it was love at first sight...oops...sorry, readers, I'm getting mushy here. I didn't mean to change the theme of this book. Anyway, on my invitation Geri came back to the island; and when she did, she stayed...for good.

This 21-year-old, lovely, strawberry blonde from California put a beach bum's heart in a spin...and...(Oh, no, here I go again). She even talked me into putting on a shiny new pair of shoes for the wedding. I still have those shoes, worn only once. My feelings for Geri definitely overpowered my wanderlust, and I soon found myself settling on an island that was moving in the opposite direction of my dreams.

Management changes at the Galleon and my new responsibility led to a new stage at...guess where (are you ready for this?)...THE HOLIDAY INN.

Yes, readers, I know what you're thinking...I wish this guy would make up his mind; does he want to be Robinson Crusoe or play in the cocktail lounge of a Holiday Inn?? Well, what can I say...Just like the island, I was also changing.

By now the once traffic free roads of George Town were becoming congested with taxis and Toyotas. And real estate agents lurked behind coconut trees looking for foreigners who could be prospective land owners. As fast as some islander could sign on the dotted line, they acquired more money than they had ever dreamed of. Some sold land that had been handed down for generations...Beach land that, at the time, seemed to have no great value; land a cow or goat wouldn't want to graze on; land that mushroomed condos...some worth $400,000 each.

THE TREASURE HUNT

I was booked to perform one day for a special beach party. Setting up instruments under tall pine trees along the beach made me an easy target for a camera-binocular-beach bag toting tourist.

"Excuse me...How far is the water from the beach?"

"How far is the water from the what?" I said.

"From the beach."

"Sir, you might wanna ask Tom over there...he's a true born Caymanian. He might know."

A few moments later, I saw Tom scratching his head as he pointed toward the vast Caribbean Sea. The pleased tourist nodded his approval.

Tom, in his mid-seventies, had the task of raking an endless rain of Australian pine needles that carpeted the white sand. With a wheelbarrow-full, Tom slowly cruised by the temporary stage area set up for the party.

"You know, Mr. George, dem tourist ask nonsense questions sometimes."

"I know, Tom, but I guess if we were visiting their home, we might be the same way."

"Not I, sir. I travel around this worl' six times on a tanka, and I never ask a fool question like dem."

Tom took a handkerchief from his pants pocket and wiped the brim of his well worn straw hat. "Once a fellow from up New Yo'k way ax's what dat is," he says, pointing towards a breadfruit tree.

"But, Tom, they don't have breadfruit in New York!!" I tried to explain.

Not hearing what I said, he went on...

"I tell 'im, it's a breadfruit; and he say, a what?? And I say breadfruit, and he say, 'ow you spell dat? Spell it, I say, we don't spell it, we eat it."

Reaching into his baggy pants pocket, Tom pulled out a gold watch and two American twenty dollar bills. "And dem so careless...see 'ere what I find rakin' dis mornin'."

"Hey, some find, Tom. Yesterday's cruise passengers must have lost it."

"I find two watches and ring las' week."

"Tom, you should open a duty free shop with all this treasure."

A slight guilty look came over his honest wrinkled face. He explained that rarely did anyone claim the lost items. By the time the valuables were missed, the owners were long gone to another island or back home, somewhere between Maine and California.

"Tom, I wouldn't worry about it; finders keepers, that's what I say."

"I don't know, Mr. George. I don't know."

The special beach party was for the Axco Chemical group. They had chartered the luxury liner, "Song of the Islands." Cayman was the final port of call after visiting Jamaica and Cozumel. The Axco Chemical company apparently had had a very profitable year, for no expense was spared to make sure the employees and their spouses had the best of times on this all expense paid Caribbean cruise.

The Cayman beach party was to be the last big beach bash before their final leg of the voyage...back to the USA. We were hired to do our regular island melodies, while turtle burgers and rum punches were served between glass bottom boat rides. The highlight of the Cayman beach party was to be "The Treasure Hunt."

Now this wasn't going to be Tom sifting sand for lost wallets. Rather it was a real live treasure hunt, with the grand prize being an actual gold doubloon and a week's vacation for two, all expenses paid, back to the Cayman Islands.

Cayman has a history of pirating, wenching, and hidden

treasures, so a treasure hunt seemed appropriate as the grand finale of this ten-day cruise. The band and I tried hard not to look rude, laughing at 450 sunburned figures playing silly beach games, like the potato sack race and toss-the-egg.

Three p.m. was the scheduled time for the big treasure hunt. By half past two, the area in front of our stage was jammed packed with anxious treasure seekers.

"Ladies and Gentlemen, welcome to the Cayman Islands," announced the cruise director over our public address system. "On Jamaica, we danced to reggae; now in the Caymanian tradition, we are going treasure hunting for a GOLD DOUBLOON." With that the oily, sweaty, sand-caked bodies dropped their turtle burgers and beach bags.

"Somewhere between the tennis courts and that tall coconut tree, we have hidden three treasures. Besides the doubloon and a Cayman Vacation, we have a second and third prize. These will of course be much easier to find."

A few more rules were explained. Then, as the countdown began, the mob went crazy with excitement. "Get on your mark, get set...GO!"

Instantly the beach turned into a cloud of dust as hysterical treasure hunters tore apart lounge chairs, uprooted bushes and climbed coconut trees in search of the hidden booty.

In no time at all, the third place prize was found, a silver wine flask, tied to a coconut tree. Soon someone screamed with delight as they found the second place prize, a case of over-proof rum. However, the biggie wasn't going to be that easy. The crowd did not leave a coral rock unturned, nor an inch of sand unsifted. Slowly the cheerful mood of the hunters became belligerent. People were now being shoved and kicked as the excitement mounted.

The doubloon was certainly well hidden. Fifteen minutes

went by and still no one discovered it. During all the goings-on, Tom was filling his wheelbarrow, paying the unthoughtful herd no mind as they trampled on his neatly raked sand.

In the meantime, we played up-tempo treasure hunting music. (What's treasure hunting music!?)

The cruise director got back on the microphone, "Okay, folks, we have winners for the third and second place prizes, but no gold doubloon yet!! Now, I'm gonna be a nice guy and help you out. Let's limit the beach area. The doubloon is somewhere between the barbecue pit and the beach bar...GOOD LUCK !!"

With that the troops bunched up closer. It was hot; the burning ultraviolet rays didn't help the situation one bit. Soon a scuffle broke out; next some senior citizen dropped of heat stroke and still...no treasure. We kept the treasure hunting music going.

"Okay, folks, it seems you're having a bit of bad luck today," said the cruise director, trying to inject some lost humor. "So because I'm a nice guy...one final clue. The treasure is somewhere between that utility pole and that green lounge chair," pointing in each direction with the final hint. With that, the crowd now condensed like sardines into an area about the size of a tennis court.

Throughout the madness, Tom had accumulated another full wheelbarrow of pine needles and other beach rubbish. It was some contrast to see Tom slowly, in typical low gear island time, half asleep, wheelbarrowing by this run-amuck mob looking for gold.

Well, folks, I don't know what made me do it... "it had to be the devil in me"...But I couldn't resist. I grabbed the microphone from the tour director and shouted...

"Did anyone check the wheelbarrow???"

"THE WHEELBARROW," someone screamed.

Well, do I need to say more? Poor, old slow-moving Tom

was demolished. As his straw hat went in one direction, pine needles and garden rake went in another. Then through the speakers, I blasted...

"The shoes, did someone check his shoes??"

Soon Tom's sneakers were flying through the air. For his age, Tom is a strong man; however, I wasn't too sure how much of this punishment he could take.

"Did anyone check the salad bowl?"

With that the Chef and his two assistants were in no better shape than Tom, who was peeling himself off the sand. The bartenders found this all just as amusing as we did so I let them have it.

"The punch bowl, did anyone check the punch bowl?"

The now out-of-control mob did a reverse, and the bartenders ran for their lives.

"Sharks in a frenzy have more manners than this bunch," I thought to myself. It was certainly an interesting study in human behavior. As Tom searched for his shoes, the Chef spat curses towards me.

In the midst of it all, some lucky lady from St. Louis finally found the gold doubloon. It was well hidden under the root of a pine tree. Wisely, she said nothing of her find until she stood on the safety of our raised stage.

Because Tom had been so good spirited about the whole hilarious incident, the cruise director awarded him a silver coin. And the not-so-lucky treasure hunters awarded him a big round of applause (after they calmed down a bit).

It was the only treasure hunt I had ever witnessed in these islands. However, legend claims the caves, reefs, and sands here hold a fortune in gold. Now I can't speak for legend, but Tom, the lucky lady from St. Louis, and I have found our treasure along the Cayman shores.

THE KING OF TREASURE HUNTERS...

I am your classic doubting Thomas. I blame it on the profession I'm in. When you deal with people who have rum flowing through their veins, they are either nicer than normal or just the complete reverse. And some vacationers have a tendency to be some of the biggest b-s-ers around. A bank teller from Fondulac, Wisconsin can tell me he's vice president of a bank, and who am I to question him?? Where's Fondulac? Now, my lovely wife, Geri, is just the opposite. In her opinion, everyone wears a white hat.

We were invited to a slide show one afternoon at a local restaurant. The invitation read:

Private Showing
Presenting the Treasures of Mel Fisher
RSVP

"Who's Mel Fisher?" I ask my always on-top-of-things, well informed wife.

"Never heard of him," she says (this was ten years before his big find), "but let's go. I'm dying for some other form of entertainment besides you."

At the small pub, a gathering of about twenty island residents were present. A local investment broker introduced us to Mel Fisher from the Florida Keys. The shy Mr. Fisher spoke very little (he didn't look like any treasure hunter to me), then he passed around a gold bar. It must have weighed 15 pounds. That's when I sensed something was up.

"Honey, let's go. They're trying to sell us something," I whispered in Geri's ear.

"Oh, come on. I want to see the slide show. I haven't seen TV or a movie since I arrived on this rock. So let's stay."

"Okay. You'll see. Watch. They're gonna try to sell us real

estate in the Florida Keys. Just watch!"

"Shhhh," said Geri, and the lights went off.

The broker narrated, and the first thing he said as an aerial shot of an island filled the screen...

"Here, ladies and gentlemen, are the Florida Keys."

I lightly nudged Geri in the ribs..."Told ya so."

"Shhhhhhhh..." said someone in the audience.

Then each slide became more interesting and harder to believe. We saw shots of Mel's treasure: chests full of gold coins, chains of silver embroidered with rubies and emeralds, cannons, swords, and more doubloons.

Then came the sales pitch. "Now folks, that was nothing compared to the treasure that sunk with the Atocha in a 1622 hurricane," said the broker.

The lights came on and before our eyes could adjust, we were handed documents filled with big, complicated, company-forming words.

"We're looking for investors," said the broker. "It takes a lot of money and endless dangerous hours of diving to search for treasure. Now you folks can become an investor in Mel Fisher's hunt for the Atocha."

I ignored the papers handed to me, but not Geri.

"Look, Honey, for a thousand dollars we can become rich when Mel finds the Atocha," said Geri.

"What's wrong with you, Geri? You're always so naive. If this guy really found all the treasure we just saw, then why is he here looking for money?"

"Oh, he looks like such a nice, honest fellow," she said.

"Yes, he is rather cute; but that's no reason to give a complete stranger one thousand dollars, one thousand dollars we don't have."

"Let's borrow it from the bank."

"No way. Get off it already. He's never gonna find that treasure. I know what I'm talking about."

"You drink a thousand dollars worth of beer in less than a year. Just give that up, lose some weight, and soon we'll be rich," my wife continued.

"No! No, forget it. I know what I'm talking about."

Well, folks, you know the rest of the story, and if there was anyone who deserved being rewarded with a several billion dollar treasure find in 1985, it was Mel Fisher. And if there was anyone who did not deserve to collect royalties from that famous find, it was I...the king of doubting Thomases. And if there was anyone who deserved to say, "I TOLD YOU SO," it was my bookkeeper, accountant, secretary, and loving wife, Geri.

Oh well, NEXT TIME, HONEY!!!

"HOW TO MANAGE AN ISLAND RESORT"

In the Caribbean, hotel managers come and go like the hurricane season. Some leave a trail of destruction, while others just roll with the flow, rarely creating a ripple in a never ending struggle to keep hotel owners, guests, and native employees happy. When I try to count the list of managers, assistant managers, controllers, chefs, bar managers and so on that have passed through these islands, I always lose count once I get past the first few years of my life in the tropics.

With each new executive came new ideas on how an island resort should be run. One of the most common theories of proper island hotel management is "personnel training." "No one has taken time to train the islanders, to show them the ropes of the trade, to lead them in the right direction..." Oh, my...how often have I heard this??? One new Cornell-trained general manager some years back put up a memo:

To all Staff:
 Starting next month, all staff are invited to join management for training classes. Classes are to be conducted in the following categories:
   Waitressing, bartending, courtesy and proper dress.
 Classes will be conducted in the main banquet room, after your shifts.
 Signed, The General Manager
 P.S. Snacks and sodas will be available.

Our new manager was rather proud of what he thought was the first effort of this type to train employees and believed he just might write a book after it was all done, entitled **How To Run An Island Resort**. The first day of class no one showed up, with the exception of one unfamiliar face.

"And you, sir, what's your name?" echoes the manager's voice in the nearly empty banquet room.

"I, Thomas," answers a tall Jamaican, while filling a plastic bag with chips and cans of orange soda.

"Thomas. Well, I'm glad you could make it. What department are you with? You don't look familiar."

"I no department, Sa. I wait for me wife. She work in kitchen. She get off in few minit."

"You don't work here, you're not employed by this hotel, and you're the only one who shows up? AND...AND... YOU'RE EATING MY FOOD!!!!!"

The boss loosened the tie on his starch-stiff shirt and stormed out of the room, nearly tripping over an electrical cord connected to a film projector.

Thomas obliviously chomped on potato chips and celery sticks, wondering to himself, *Wat wrong wit' dat crazy foreigner?*

Back in his office, the new manager ordered his secretary to re-do the memo and this time take note...class attendance is not a request...it's MANDATORY. She does as she is told and distributes the memo.

Next day a good portion of bartenders, waitresses, and front desk personnel do not show up for work, much less for class. While our new overworked boss waits tables, a senior-official from the local immigration department waits for him in the executive office. Between the breakfast and lunch crowd, he has time for a fast meeting.

"Yes, I have to make this fast...most of my staff didn't show up today. What can I do for you?"

"Sir, most of your staff is down at my office filing complaints to have you deported."

"Deported...DEPORTED?? Why? What's the problem?"

"They tell us you want them to stay extra hours after their shift, without pay. Is that true?"

Sinking into his giant chair like a deflated balloon, the manager explains his reasoning behind the classes and how the staff would benefit by attending them. The immigration official apparently wasn't listening or just couldn't care less.

"Sir, I advise you to pay the staff overtime if you intend for them to stay after their shift."

"Overtime? I'm going to give them free training experience...experience that has taken me years to learn, and I should pay them overtime??"

"Well, sir, you do whatever you like. I'm only giving you advice from my experience. Don't forget you're just passing through our fair island...best not be too pushy."

"Pushy? PUSHY? I'm trying to help these...Oh, forget it. Excuse me. I have to get back to work."

With that pow-wow to add to the already sh--y day in paradise, our perturbed new boss was back to work—this time mixing drinks at the beach bar. As he apologized to a few guests for any inconvenience caused due to shortage of staff, a few of his non-working bartenders ordered a round of exotic island drinks. These contain about a dozen variations of rums and liqueurs. Their recipes cannot be found, even in the most updated Bartenders Guide. Anything beyond a scotch and water had the new chief bewildered and the non-working bartenders knew this.

"You want a what?" said the slightly embarrassed boss.

"A Tropical Sunrise, wit' two cherry an' slice of pineapple."

"I wan' a Bahama Mama," said another islander.

Soon a crowd of domino-playing natives got into the action of ordering drinks that normally only tourists request.

"Me, I wan' a Planta-punch." "I wan' a Honeymoon Special." "One Splice-the-Main-Brace over here." Sarcastic chuckles followed each order.

After a scan through the endless assortment of rainbow colored bottles, the new boss, in disgust, threw his hands into the air and admitted he was lost and had no idea where to start. With a trace of tropical ridicule, one of the non-working bartenders said, "Okay, den how about four Bacardi and ginger, and if you want, we can have a class tomorrow after your shift, an' teach you how to make da tropical drinks."

With that the defeated boss got the point and a few days later all was back to normal. The office memo on training classes was hidden away in the good-try file and chapter one on how to run an island resort has yet to be written.

THE TRAYS

In my opinion, a successful hotel manager in the Caribbean must have a sense of humor. You've got to take time out to laugh.

This point might seem unimportant; however, after almost 20 years of hanging around tropical resorts, I've come to the conclusion that this is the key to surviving the slow mode of the tropics when one is trained to be aggressive, punctual and in authority. Take time to laugh at all the confusion. Laugh at your sleeping security guards, your comic book reading hostesses, and your leaking two hundred thousand dollar swimming pool. That's just da way it goes in da Islands. There's no way you can follow North American or European standards of hotel management in the tropics. The numerous ex-patriot experts who have been carried off islands in straight-jactets are proof of this.

For example...If you fire a waitress for sleeping on the job, she will move to the hotel next door and get another job. The waitress who replaces her just got fired from the same hotel next door (the one your fired waitress went to work at). And your replacement was fired by the hotel next door for "sleepin' on the job." If it sounds like a catch-22...IT IS!!

One evening a newly arrived general manager stormed into the hotel's kitchen. He was not in the best of moods.

"Who's doing room service tonight?" he shouted.

"I, Sa," said the young female dressed in tennis shoes, rolled up jeans and T-shirt.

"You, what kind of uniform is that? What does that T-shirt say?"

The manager read out loud, "The Palms Hotel and Beach Club. This is how you're dressed for room service? Couldn't you at least advertise the hotel you collect a weekly salary from??"

"Wat wrong wit dis? I get dis free from The Palms; you only give da touris' free T-shirt."

"Never mind that, you shouldn't wear T-shirts, jeans, and tennis shoes to work anyway. Where is your uniform?"

"Uniform...dat bogus lookin' ding. I not wearin' dat!!"

"Look...just...oh, never mind...I want all the trays removed from the hotel lobbies."

"Trays, sa? Wat trays?"

"The room service trays. When guests finish eating they set them outside their doors. Leaving them there overnight is unhealthy, it attracts bugs and it looks bad."

"But sa, I just start me shift. Dat was left from da las' shift so why should..."

"I don't care whose shift it is, just get the trays out of the lobby," interrupted a now-frustrated boss.

"Okay, sa. Okay, I take care of it."

"And not tomorrow. NOW!!"

The German chef got a stern look from a displeased manager as he stormed out of the hot, stuffy kitchen. The chef knew he'd be called into the office the next morning for this oversight. Shaking in his wooden clogs, he started to moan, "I can't do everything. I can't prepare food, worry about room service trays, uniforms and keeping stock. When I worked in Toronto, I never had to stand over a hot stove. I just worked out of my office and my efficient staff got their jobs done."

A distant voice from the dishwashing area shouted "Den why you no back in Toronto?"

"Who said that?" said the chef, dropping his giant soup spoon.

"Chef, just forget it. I need three lobster tails," says the Italian maitre d'.

"Lobster tails? Didn't anyone tell you we're out of lobster tails?"

"No lobster tails? This is an order for the manager, his wife and the owner...What do I tell them?"

"Tell them, tell them the boat didn't come, customs hasn't cleared the papers, the season is closed, the usual stuff."

"You're nuts. He's not in the best of moods today...you tell him yourself."

The chef took twenty dollars from his pocket and ordered his native assistant to run to the hotel next door and buy three lobster tails.

"And make it fast," said the chef.

"Alright, sir, dat a good idea," said the assistant as he dropped his apron and rushed out the back door.

The maitre d' started to laugh.

"What's so funny? You got any better ideas?" said the chef.

"Great idea, chef. Great idea, except you'll never see him again tonight."

"Why? He's got my twenty dollars."

"That's right, and there's a big beach dance next door. So you're out an assistant, out twenty dollars, and still out of lobster."

The manager, his wife, and the owner had a dinner of pork chops, while an apologetic chef was on his knees begging for mercy.

A check was made on the room service trays. Just as the boss had ordered, the trays were removed...but dirty forks, knives, plates, and napkins were left behind.

THE RAISE

Mr. and Mrs. Sutton, a management husband and wife team, had a better theory when they arrived to run a small 75-room resort on the northern end of the island. The first thing the Suttons did was hand out raises.

Now this was the way to get the islanders on your side. This would help in forming a team. Teamwork...that's how to run an island resort. Now what better way to form a team than by giving everyone a raise right from the start. The longer one has been employed at the hotel, the bigger the raise...(naturally)

KNOCK-KNOCK.

"Please come in," answered Mr. Sutton as he sifted through a mass of paperwork left by the last booted-out manager.

In walked three charming, elderly ladies wearing pink uniforms and straw hats. They made up the total of his laundry room staff.

"Ladies, Ladies, good morning...what can I do for you?" He removed files from a spring exposed couch and offered his employees a seat.

"Sir, yesterday you give me ten extra dolla' in de envelope," said the obvious leader of the trio.

"Yes, ma'am, that's your raise. Everyone working here received a raise," said a proud, glowing manager.

"But my two cousin here who work with me, dey only got five dollar, sir."

"That's because you've been working here much longer than they have, ma'am, so you get a bigger raise."

"But sir, that's not right. If I get ten dolla', dey should too get ten dolla'."

"Ladies, ladies..."

Before he had a chance to re-explain, the trio walked out and went home.

That evening a baffled Mr. and Mrs. Sutton were doing laundry when they should have been hosting guests in the dining room. News of the inconsiderate manager spread throughout the small north end village. And this of course made the task of finding replacements for the laundry impossible. A want ad in the classified section of the weekly paper proved fruitless. Soon the Suttons gave in, hired the three laundry ladies back and gave the two cousins ten extra dollars.

When the trio returned, dirty laundry was stacked to the

ceiling. They worked extra long hours to take care of the accumulated towels, sheets, table cloths, and staff uniforms. They worked on their off days, and even during lunch breaks. On the following payday, the skeptical boss, in no mood for more possible unrest, added overtime pay along with their ten dollar raise.

KNOCK-KNOCK.

"Come in please," said Mr. Sutton. To his shock it was the three ladies from the laundry room.

"Ladies, please...OH, NO, what did I do wrong?"

"You make a mistake, sir." They dropped the overtime money on his desk and went back to work.

NOW THAT'S TYPICAL TROPICAL
WHEN YOU LIVIN' IN THE SUN
THAT'S TYPICAL TROPICAL
DON'T WORRY MON SOON COME
WE GET CHRISTMAS CARDS IN JUNE
GO CRAZY IN FULL MOON
BUT THAT'S TYPICAL, TYPICAL TROPICAL

From the Song TYPICAL TROPICAL

VIII

Off To The Big Island—AMERICA

At the time of this writing, I figure I've made approximately 4,700 nightly performances in the Cayman Islands. During these performances, seventy-five percent of my repertoire has been the same line-up of tunes, the Caribbean classics, the ones I've mentioned over and over again...Yellow Bird, Island in the Sun, Matilda, etc.

I am often asked, "How can you do it...night after night, the same routine?" There are three reasons why I've been able to keep a smile on my face and not go bananas.

First of all, I love it. So few people really truly love the work they do—I even find it hard to call my job "work." Secondly, although my repertoire remains basically the same, the audience changes constantly. Every week the hotel turns over a new flock of visitors. The third reason is "Harry."

Harry is the show within the show. He has been my bass player and limbo dancer since 1973. I will never get bored with Harry in my band. He is definitely one of a kind...the jack of all trades and master of a few (like making excuses)...and a legend in his own mind.

There are thousands of "Harry Stories," and I know the Harry fans are going to come to me and say, "Why didn't you write this one or that one." Well, to include all of these tales would take a separate book, so I have listed just some of the favorites. These stories take place off-island or as some island residents say...on the mainland..."da big island of America."

Before I start, however, let me explain a few things—first the "Great Expectations Syndrome." Have you ever gone to a strange city or country and visualized ahead of time what it would be like? For example, when I first landed in Oahu, Hawaii, I was expecting only grass shacks, outrigger canoes and brown-skinned topless girls with flowers in their hair. And on arrival to America from Germany as a young boy, I expected cowboys and Indians just like in the western movies I'd seen. That's what I call the "Great Expectations Syndrome."

Then there's the whole, strange, out-of-place combination of Harry and me: we are truly a musical odd-couple. Here's Harry, a West Indian who, like most West Indians, is full of natural talent. He's a superb bass player, a good dancer, and an excellent singer. Then there's me. I can't dance, I know just three or four chords on the guitar, and my singing (Uhmmm...well)—that's a matter of opinion.

Yet, I'm the foreigner in the West Indies who sings the calypsos and reggaes and leads the band. It just doesn't fit...It would be like a black rasta-man from the islands leading a polka band in an alpine-resort in the Swiss mountains.

Once I said to Harry, "You should sing more, learn a few more songs." Harry responds with, "Jawg, me no want make you look bad, so I betta not sing too much."

Next, keep in mind that until the mid-1970s, life in the Cayman Islands was laid back, much like an indefinite siesta. With the exception of the men who went off to sea, few islanders were exposed to anything beyond the shores of the island.

Around the middle of 1975, we were made an offer by

a real estate developer, Cecil Fox, to fly to Chicago to perform for a show tagged, "CAYMAN NIGHT." The idea...to sell Cayman, to bring more tourists to the island, and of course for Cecil to sell beach property.

By now I had a full band with drummer, guitarist, extra vocalist and of course the star, "Harry." Mr. Fox gave us enough cash for five round-trip air tickets to Chicago and a guarantee that more money, food, and accommodations would be waiting on our arrival.

We were all very excited. It was to be Harry's and Philip's first trip to America. Philip was extremely shy. He lived in his own little shell and inside that shell all he cared about was his guitar. Give him a song and his guitar and "WOW"; all that's shelled up inside comes bursting through his fingers on the fretboard. Philip "Smiley" Bodden is an unbelievable talent who enjoys a reputation as one of the finest guitarists in the islands.

There was no rush to get to Chicago, so we took part of our travel money and rented a large station wagon. We decided to drive the route (Miami-Chicago) instead of fly. I wanted Harry and Philip to the see that great country called "A..erica."

Don Foster travelled with us. Don is a character in his own right, who nowadays is the chief of the successful DON FOSTER'S DIVING in Grand Cayman. At that time, though, he was my drummer.

Also coming along for the ride was Alberto, the drink-mixing expert. In exchange for a free ticket, he was to blend island concoctions at the Cayman party.

The final member of this group was Andy "The Cayman Cowboy" Martin, an Islander who sang country and western. He always added a special novelty to our show. Andy had been around the world a few times as a merchant-seaman working aboard giant oil tankers.

Andy, Don, Alberto and myself had all done our share of traveling. We could each look at a map and find Chicago, Canada, or Alaska. But not so Harry and Philip. They hadn't the faintest idea of how big the United States was. To them, it was just another island...bigger of course, but just another island.

For them, the major difference lay in the fact that this island called America was full of stars. That's where all those folks lived that starred in the movies and sang on the record albums...which brings us back to the "Great Expectations Syndrome."

Phillip hardly spoke throughout our entire trip. He never expressed his expectations. He just sort of sat in the station wagon, looking like a mannequin, staring out the window for the whole 2,000 mile journey. I don't know whether he was scared or mesmerized. It was probably both.

The most exciting thing he said was when we were going through immigration in Miami, "Uh, Barefoot, are we going to take a taxi to Chicago?"

As for Harry...well, the best way to explain his "Great Expectations Syndrome" is to imagine all of America as two city blocks. One block is nothing but Hollywood and the other is Motown Records.

While we were waiting for the courtesy mini-bus to take us to our rental car at Miami's busy International Airport, Philip gazed about in disbelief as his eyes watered from a first contact with pollution. I counted baggage, guitars, and money while Andy, Alberto, and Don started picking on Harry.

"Harry, look over there, it's John Wayne," said Don.

"That's not John Wayne," said Andy, "that's Clint Eastwood."

"Looks more like Bruce Lee to me," added Alberto.

They were getting Harry excited and soon he had just

spotted his first star. "Jawg, Jawg, look Trini Lopez...Trini Lopez."

"Trini Lopez, you mean the Latin singer?"

"Yes, dat 'im...LOOK, LOOK!"

I looked through the crowd while Don and Andy did a poor Trini Lopez imitation, singing "La La La Bamba."

"Harry, you're nuts. There's no Trini Lopez."

"Da man wit da red shirt. Look, Trini Lopez."

"Listen to me, Harry. There's millions of Latins in Miami. They all look alike...that's not Trini Lopez."

"Hey, watch it, senor," said Alberto, a short, hot-tempered Latin himself.

To get back at me for my (intended to be joking) racist remark, Alberto patted Harry on the back and said, "You know Harry, that does look like Trini Lopez."

"You see, Jawg, I tell you...Trini Lopez."

Behind Harry's back, Alberto grinned at me. Andy confirmed the identification, agreeing it could be Trini Lopez. Figuring Alberto, Andy, and Don were also spotting celebrities, Harry was now on a roll.

"You see, Jawg, I got his album. Dat 'ow I know it 'im."

What could I say? It was four against one. Philip stayed neutral and bewildered.

Before the courtesy bus arrived, Harry also spotted Jimmy Buffet, Aretha Franklin and several other stars whose albums he had back home. But the best one was...Lou Rawls.

"Jawg, der, over der look, Lou Rawls, Lou Rawls."

I spotted Harry's Lou Rawls. It was a skycap!! On his handcart, he had a guitar case along with a few other pieces of luggage.

We headed north on I-95 with country music blasting on the radio. Harry was slowly calming down from the shower of stars.

"Let's stop and get some beer," said Alberto.

"Ya, and some cheeseburgers," added Don.

Don, who weighed somewhere between 200 and 250 pounds could easily down a half-dozen burgers and fries, topped with a few chocolate shakes. And Alberto and Andy could easily take in the same amount of calories in the form of liquor.

Somewhere between Miami and Fort Lauderdale, I made an exit off I-95 and pulled into the first store, a 7-11. Harry bought everything in sight—Kung-fu magazines, shampoo, deodorant, Slurpees...

"Man, wat a deal. Look, Jawg!"

Harry was loaded down with junk. This was his first taste of American shopping, his first taste of reasonable prices. I grabbed a few six-packs, Philip bought a "Guitar Player" magazine and Don walked across the street to the golden arches to load up with food.

Back on the road again, Harry took inventory: hair net, shower cap, matches, key chain and a large assortment of after-shave lotions, body creams and so on.

"Harry, why did you buy all that junk? Can't you wait till we get to Chicago?" I asked.

Philip interrupted his own silence, "Isn't this Chicago?"

Harry said, "Jawg, man, it a good deal...look dis Right Guard only 99 cents. In Cayman it two dolla."

"Ya," said Andy. "That's a good deal, so leave him alone, Barefoot."

Gee, strike two...I lose again.

With about 400 miles behind us, we were running low on munchies. "Get off at the next exit," said Alberto. "We need more beer."

I got off the highway, turned onto the first main road, and there was another 7-11. This is no big deal to anyone who lives or travels in America...these mini-markets are every-

where. And I gave it no second thought as we went directly to the large fridge to get our resupply of brew. Harry,
however, walked about the store in amazement. He knew
we had just traveled some six hours, but there was the same
magazine rack, the same Slurpee machine, the same
telephone booth, all in the same places as our last stop.

"Jawg, Jawg, I 'ate to tell you dis."

"What is it, Harry?"

"Jawg, man, you been going in circles. Dis the same store."

With no help from Don or Andy, who promptly suggested
I check the road map, I finally explained to Harry that this
was an enterprising country he was being exposed to, and
he best get used to seeing the same 7-11s, golden arches,
and Shell oil signs wherever we went.

We stopped for a night's rest after crossing the Georgia
state line. As I checked us into a Holiday Inn, Harry stared
at a 7-11 store across the street.

"I don't know, Jawg. I don't know. I 'ope you know where
you goin'."

I showed Philip and Harry their room. "Philip, this is a
TV," I said, turning on the wonder box. With guitar in one
hand and suitcase in the other, Philip stood directly in front
of the screen in absolute astonishment.

"Take your jacket off, Philip, and relax. See these
numbers? That's what you turn to get other channels."

I don't believe he heard me; he never moved. Harry
dropped his bags and followed us to the small cocktail
lounge. We got our share of stares from the truck drivers
and other patrons. A group consisting of a Jamaican, a
Costa Rican, a German and a 250 pound Caymanian drummer was certainly an odd sight in southern Georgia.

"Jawg, when we goin' shoppin'?"

"Harry, I told you it's best to wait till we get to Chicago.
There you can shop all you want."

"Dis not Chicago?" he asked.

"No, Harry, we've got a long way to go. Besides that, you don't need to buy any more junk. Stop wasting your money."

"I want to buy a tree-piece suit."

"A three-piece suit? For what, Harry. . .it's too hot to wear in Cayman. We don't use them as band uniforms. Why do you need a three-piece suit?"

"Me friend tell me you can get a good deal on tree-piece suits 'ere," he answered.

"Well, it's your money, Harry. Do what you want; but right now we're a long way from any shopping malls, and it's too late anyway. I'm going to bed. Good night, guys."

As I walked down the corridor toward my room, I noticed Philip's room door ajar. I was about to shut it when I saw the statue in front of the television set. It was Philip, still gazing wide-eyed at the set while the national anthem was coming over the air. His guitar was still in one hand and his suitcase was in the other. He hadn't removed his jacket or even moved an inch from the spot where I had left him several hours ago.

I rotated him, sat him on the edge of the bed, turned the channel to a late movie and said good night.

Early the next morning, I knocked on everyone's door to wake them. Harry's bloodshot eyes peeked through the opening.

"How's Philip? Did he ever sleep?" I asked.

Harry let me in. There on the edge of the bed, just where I had left him, Philip was half sitting, half lying down, guitar in one hand, suitcase in the other, snoring away. He still had his jacket and shoes on, and the TV was hissing over the snowy screen.

Soon we were on the road again. For the next few hundred miles, no one said much of anything. Then a giant 18-wheeler truck roared past us, almost picking us off the road with its invisible wake of air.

"Jawg, you know dat car you 'ave in Cayman? If I had it 'ere right now, I could drive it under da trailer of dat truck." This woke everyone, except Alberto, who was healing a hangover.

"Harry, why don't you just shut up for the rest of this trip?" said Andy.

"What, you gone mad, Harry!" laughed Don, with his belly shaking like Jello. Philip never took his eyes off the window but gave a disapproving shake of the head.

"I bet, I bet," shouted Harry.

"You bet what, Harry? You wanna bet that you can drive a small sports car under that monster 18-wheeler doing 70 miles per hour? Harry, you're coconuts!"

Alberto, sitting beside Harry in the back seat, awakened to the shouting and mixed himself a drink.

The argument went on for nearly thirty minutes, with everyone except Alberto and Philip trying to convince Harry the feat was impossible; it just couldn't be done.

Soon, Don and Andy wisely gave up. Of course, I had to keep arguing. I couldn't let Harry believe he had won this silly argument, too. While Harry went on and on, IT HIT ME. Harry had seen someone do this in a movie, either James Bond or Burt Reynolds. Yes, that was it.

"Okay, Harry, admit it. You saw someone do that in the movies." Don, Andy and even Philip agreed.

"Wat movie, wat you mean?" asked Harry.

"Come on, Harry. Give me a break. I know you. You saw James Bond drive under a big truck in a movie, so you think you can do it."

"No, Jawg, I can do it. Wanna bet?"

Alberto, still saying nothing, fixed another cocktail. As more miles passed, I did my very best to explain how stunt men in Hollywood do their tricks. I went into how they do the action very slowly, and then speed up the film to make it look real. I told Harry everything I knew about editing and splicing film. (You see I'd been on a tour at Universal Studios, and they showed us tourists how it was done.)

Harry listened and I figured for once, I was getting through to him. But not Harry. He was not going to admit he was wrong. "Na, Jawg, you wrong. You just jealous. If I 'ad you car 'ere right now, I..."

By now I had a sore throat, and his stubbornness was getting to me. Maybe if just one more person backed me...With eyes blazing into the rearview mirror, I screamed to Alberto, "Alberto, would you tell this clown...IT CANNOT BE DONE."

Alberto, mixing his third bloody-mary of the morning, spoke for the first time. "You know, I've been listening to this for the last hour and, I think he can do it."

STRIKE THREE, I'm out.

Alberto patted Harry on the back and gave me another vengeful grin in the mirror. Don and Andy snickered over the whole situation, while even stern-faced Philip cracked a smile. As for myself, "no more Latin jokes."

We had a great time in Chicago, the show went well and Harry frenzied in the fabulous shopping malls. He must have bought ten three-piece suits, a dozen pairs of those high rise shoes, hats complete with rhinestones, and everything else that had a discount price sticker attached to it.

What did it matter if he never had a chance to wear the suits back in the Islands..."It a good deal, Jawg!...It a good deal." Philip did some shopping also, buying every Jimmy Hendrix and Chet Atkins album in the city.

After a long weekend in Chicago, we were back in Miami with a few days to "play tourist" before returning to the Islands. Harry was ready to go home. He had no intentions of hanging around south Florida. HE WAS BROKE.

Alberto and I gave Harry a lift to the airport. We were dressed in our usual island attire...T-shirts, shorts, and flip-flops. In the back seat sat Harry, looking like the richest, most prosperous, best-dressed pimp in the city of Miami, adorned in a white three-piece suit, pink shirt, felt hat, high rise shoes, topped off with gold chains, four or five rings, bracelets, and of course, sunglasses. Yes, he was now a star. He had performed in America, the island of stars, the island of Trini Lopez, Aretha Franklin and Lou Rawls.

I must admit, Harry looked outstanding. "You look sharp, Harry," I said, offering a shake of my hand.

"Tanks, Barefoot," he said, beaming with pride.

We were almost at the airport when Harry tapped me on the shoulder. "STOP, STOP, magic shop, magic shop."

"What magic shop? Where?"

"Der. Look across da street. I wan' buy some tings for me show. Pull over der, Jawg."

"Okay, but make it fast, Harry. You've got a flight to catch."

"No problem, no problem," said Harry, as I pulled into the parking lot of a small shopping arcade.

Inside Juan's Magic and Novelty Shop sat Juan, a fat, cigar-smoking Cuban wearing a perspiration stained T-shirt and drinking thick black coffee.

"You 'ave dem cards dat do tricks?" asked Harry.

"Cards to do tricks? Si, senor," he said and handed Harry a deck of magic cards.

"You 'ave da magic stick, dat turn into scarf?"

"Si, senor," and he handed Harry a magic wand that turned into a scarf.

"You 'ave the metal rings you touch togeter and dey lock up like chain?"

"Magic metal rings? Si, senor," he responded and handed Harry a box of magic metal rings.

"'ow about da plastic ice cube with the fly inside?"

I interrupted, "I don't believe this. Come on, Harry. You're gonna be late. You don't need any more junk!"

"Wait, one more ting. Da hat, da magic hat, you pull da rabbit out of...you 'ave dat?"

"Hat, hat, a magician's hat...right here, senor. Anything else?" he smiled, showing tobacco-stained teeth.

Harry, with a baffled look, examined the hat, inside and out. He held it up, held it down, then turned it around a few times.

"Something wrong, senor?" asked Juan.

Harry, looking mystified, said, "Where da rabbit is, sir?"

We dropped Harry at the airport, along with a collection of cardboard boxes (West Indian luggage). He was penniless and in need of a porter so we offered our assistance.

We were some sight; Harry leading the way in this three-piece suit, shades, and hat looking like a million dollars, while Alberto and I, dressed like a couple of beach-bums, followed closely behind with his boxes.

People stared, and some whispered, "Who is that handsome black dude? Is he some sort of a star? He must be...look at those two white boys carrying his luggage."

Harry picked up on the attention. "Come on, guys, me got a plane to catch," he said, with a slight command in his voice.

Exhausted, we dropped his things at the Cayman Airways counter. People all around us were mumbling...."Gee, look at all that gold on his fingers." "Wow, that suit must have cost two hundred dollars."

Harry not only looked like a star at that moment, he was the star and the stir his presence created made him shine. After presenting his ticket, the agent said, "Thank you, Mr. Johnston, that will be $2.50 departure tax, please."

"Wat?" said Harry, looking rather surprised.

"Two dollars and fifty cents, sir, for Government Departure

tax."

Harry fumbled through the pockets of this three-piece suit...

'Sir, please, there's a large line behind you, two dollars and fifty cents departure tax."

We knew Harry's pockets were empty; he had just spent his last dime at Juan's Magic shop. Not about to admit he was broke in front of his newly acquired admirers, he patted himself all over searching for cash that wasn't there.

I sensed by the look on his face and the quiver in his voice that he was about to make up some fantastic story about a stolen wallet or a lost gold American Express Card. So, before I let Harry get the best of the situation once again, I gave the ticket agent a five dollar bill in plain view of everyone—and quickly walked away.

"Keep the change, Harry, but don't forget to pay me back," I shouted.

It's hard to get one over on Harry, but when he was standing there insolvent, my change in his hands, amongst the snickering crowd, I thought, "I did it."

Well, I almost did it.

"Jawg, Jawg, next time make sure you 'ave all this taken care of before I come to de airport."

Did he say that or was it my imagination?

Since that first trip, we have performed in almost every major city in the U.S. Philip learned how to change channels. But it took a long time for him to get over his shyness. He was always afraid to ask questions, or even answer his room telephone.

One morning we were having breakfast at the Hyatt Regency Hotel in Dallas. The night before we had performed for a Scuba Diving convention. Harry, Andy and I were on our way to Las Vegas for a short holiday. Philip planned to return to the Islands. The thought of traveling all alone had him extremely worried.

"Look, Philip, it's no big deal," I said.

"Uh, but, uh...how do I know what plane to get on when I reach Atlanta?" he asked.

"Philip, it's right here on your ticket, flight 229—Eastern Airlines to Miami."

"Uh, but...I...well..."

"Okay, Philip, I'll tell you what I'll do. Let me write all the instructions down for you, then you just check the list at every airport. You can't go wrong."

"Uh, but...I...well," he responded.

I started writing Philip's itinerary:

1. At Dallas-Fort Worth Airport go to the Braniff counter. Look at their TV screen and see what gate flight 734 to Atlanta departs from.

2. Go to that gate, board plane, sit down, fasten seat belt.

3. In Atlanta, go to the Eastern Airlines counter.

As I was writing, I explained everything verbally.

"TV screen? What channel is it on?" asked Philip, looking more frightened than ever.

"No, no, Philip, it's not on a regular TV screen...well, then, again, it is...it's..." I could see this wasn't going to work. "Look, Philip, when you get to Atlanta, just ask your stewardess to show you what gate to go to."

"Uh, oh, you mean I gotta speak to her?"

"Ya...WHAT'S THE BIG DEAL?"

Philip's home island (Cayman Brac) has a population of less than 2,000. Now for the first time he had to face America alone. He was terrified.

"Relax, Philip, we'll think of something—if you don't want to speak, you don't have to. Speak, speak! That's it!" I got a fresh piece of paper and wrote:

Hello Stewardess:

My name is Philip Bodden. I am a deaf-mute. My final destination is George Town, Grand Cayman Island. Could you be so kind as to assist me to my gate? Thank you.

I gave the note to Philip and instructed him to say nothing during the entire flight home. Just keep passing the note and ticket along to any stewardess he might see on the plane or in the airport, but say nothing. Philip liked the idea, and the whole plan helped calm him down.

I placed a long distance call to Cayman the next day to make sure Philip had arrived safely. All had gone as planned. Not only was he escorted to all his gates, he was allowed to board early and rode first-class all the way home in the company of lovely stewardesses.

"Gee," I thought. "I've got to try that trick myself one day."

"HARRY"—Bass player, limbo dancer, and star of the show.

IX

Harry Da Star

A short, approximately 40 minutes, plane ride from Grand Cayman are the so-called sister islands, Cayman Brac and Little Cayman.

Little Cayman, 11 miles long with a population under 30, can only be described with one overused word...unspoiled. It has loads of beaches, top-notch bone fishing, and breathtaking diving on virgin reefs. Offering no restaurants, classy hotels, or golf courses (at least not so far), the island appeals to those few who see beauty in seeing no one.

Then there's Cayman Brac. A visit there is like going back in time. It's Grand Cayman twenty years ago. Many Brackers feel neglected. They receive a very light trickle of tourists and near nil development of any kind as compared to Grand Cayman.

Brackers may feel neglected but, personally, I think they're lucky. Life on this twelve-mile-long island is slow and un-hectic.

At least once a year I perform there. The band and I never make any money, but usually the air tickets, a place to sleep, and good local food are all complimentary, so who cares? We always have a good time.

You're never treated as a stranger on the Brac. People will invite you to their homes, you'll be fed and entertained with stories of the sea, turtle schooners and the great storm of "'32".

Cayman Brac has a population of less that 2,000. It has a bluff on its east end, rising 140 feet, and it has very few really good beaches. But that's okay. It has charm...loads of it.

From the time I sang my first calypso song, I've traveled around the world performing in such places as the Plaza in New York and the Riviera in Las Vegas, however, my favorite spot is the Lagoon Bar on Cayman Brac. It's located right along the Brac's coral rocky shore. It's built of cement blocks and stained plywood. It's not square, yet it's not rectangular shaped. It's certainly not round or triangular. It's just sort of, well, sort of nailed together. It's neat.

In the middle of the dance floor there used to be a coconut tree. A hole had been cut into the roof to give the tree plenty of breathing space. In one corner sits an old rusting juke box with broken speakers and loads of good country records. The patrons sit on bench-style seats; however, most just stand around and mingle.

There was no wind this particular night we performed there and, of course, no air-conditioning. The shutters around the club were all open, held up with sturdy bamboo poles. The place was jammed-packed with locals and a few dozen tourists. Now jammed packed at the Lagoon Bar means around 100 bodies, plus an additional 200 or so hanging around outside.

We always change our song line up on the Brac. Instead of the regular tourist-type music, we switch to mostly uptempo murangees and lots of country. So we fill the night with Hank Williams, George Jones, and Freddy Fender. Not neglecting the visitors, however, we have a special added attraction: Harry doing his "broken bottle dance." "And now, ladies and gentlemen, here he is, the Voodoo Man himself...HARRY," I announced on this particular visit. Only the tourists applauded. The locals wanted to dance. They were in no mood for Harry's tourist-pleasing show. The faster it was over, the faster they could get back on the dance floor. The Brackers patiently sat out Harry's performance.

Harry took about two dozen empty beer bottles, broke them all by pounding one bottle against another. He then danced around and over the broken glass. We increased the tempo, and the tourists started clapping along in time. Harry now began jumping like some Watusi Warrior. Then the drums rolled and Harry took a frog-leap into the air, landing bare feet first on the broken glass.

A hush fell over the audience, then an OOOOOOOH, followed by applause. Harry now stomped his feet into the broken glass. He rubbed the glass in his face and behind his ears. He laid on the smashed bottles and had a big lady come from the audience to step on him, adding pressure against the sharp splinters. The tempo again increased; the clapping got louder. Now Harry did a yoga-type headstand on the broken glass. The tourists loved it. All two dozen gave Harry a standing ovation. Harry bowed, and the show was over.

"Folks, we're going to take a short intermission now. As soon as Harry changes (and sweeps up the glass), we have more dance music."

This time the Brackers clapped.

After a fast change of clothes, Harry returned to the jammed, steamy bar. Immediately he was swarmed by a group of tourists who shook his hand and patted his back in reward for the fascinating show. Harry, of course, loved the attention, eating up each compliment like a starving dog.

"Music, music," shouted an islander.

"Gimme break now, mohn," snapped back Harry.

"How do you do that?" asked one inquisitive tourist.

"Yeah, what's the secret, Harry?" asked another.

"It voodoo. I learn fom da voodoo man in hills of Jamaica," said Harry.

The visitors of course were impressed with this.

"Voodoo...gee...so you know voodoo...wow."

Harry, beaming from all the attention, said, "Yes, and it dangerous ting to do."

"Have you ever been cut?" asked the big lady who stood on Harry.

"No...never get cut, only get cut if someone 'ave lime in dey pocket."

"What? Did you say lime?" asked the big lady.

"Dat right, lime. If anyone 'ave lime in dey pocket while I do show, I cut up me foot bottom bad."

"Wow!"

"Gee!"

"OOOOOHHHH!"

Hearing the b-s Harry was laying on the naive tourists had us barstool-sitting patrons mystified.

My friend, Ried Dennis said, "George, you never told me about the lime."

"Hey, Harry has been doing that show once a week for the last umpteen years and that's the first time I heard about it myself."

At the end of the evening, as we were packing up instruments, I asked Harry about the lime.

"Harry, how could you give those poor innocent tourists all that baloney about the lime?"

"Wat baloney? Dat true, you know. If anyone 'ave lime in dey pocket, I cut me foot on da bottom bad."

"So, Harry, how come over all these years you've never mentioned that before?"

"You never ax."

"Harry, you're too much...too much."

"Jawg, you too jealous."

A week later we were back on Grand Cayman—it was Wednesday night, the night Harry does his glass-dance. Of course, by now all the regular lounge customers had been told about the Harry-Lime story. We were on our second intermission. Harry was off in his changing room preparing for the show when the bartender had a great idea.

"Here, everybody take a piece of lime, put it in your pocket and move up close to the stage area when Harry does his performance."

A dozen or so of us gathered around the bar, each taking a piece of lime from a small plastic cup. The lime is always there, used for mixing vodka tonics, margaritas or whatever. We chuckled over the trick we were about to play on Harry; and by show time, nearly a dozen people had joined in our little prank.

Harry went through the routine we'd seen hundreds of times: smashed bottles, danced, leapt, and so on. Tonight the locals who normally paid the show no mind were all gathered around the stage area, watching, applauding, and cheering Harry along (each one had a piece of lime in his pocket). The show finished with no signs of blood. Anxiously, we waited for Harry's return from his changing room.

"We got him this time," said Don the drummer. "He'll never swindle out of this one."

"Ha...I can't wait to see his face when we show him the lime," said the bartender.

Harry entered the room and I called him over.

"Harry, that was a good show. Now tell us again about the lime; some of the folks haven't heard it."

"Well, da only way me cut me foot-bottom is if someone 'ave lime in dey pocket...and den me get cut bad."

While Harry talked, we reached into our pockets. Each one of us produced a piece of lime. Holding it between two fingers, we shoved it towards Harry's nose. Harry's eyes widened, his jawbone dropped, and his words turned into blubbering.

The bartender, obviously very proud of his jest, said, "Well, Harry, we were all watching. We saw no blood. Why didn't you get cut?"

We all snickered, awaiting Harry's response.

"NO, NO," said Harry. "It 'ave to be a WHOLE LIME." With that he walked away...once again the victor.

THE MYSTERY LADY

It started as just another typical-tropical evening. I showed up about an hour before our nightly performance, tuned my guitar, checked the sound system, and downed a few cups of coffee with the hotel's night manager.

"We have a television film crew coming into the lounge tonight," said the night manager.

"Oh yeah? For anything special?" I asked.

"A tourism promotion film. The exposure should be good for the hotel."

"Okay, that's great. I'll see to it Harry is in top form for his limbo show tonight."

"Yes, they would like to film the band performing a few hot calypsos and then Harry, complete with fire and limbo."

Harry's speciality is the Limbo-Fire dance. The glass dance is nice, but there's something exotic about the Limbo. The blend of a fast calypso-drum beat, fire blazing from the limbo pole, and Harry's bright colorful costume is always a special treat for our visitors.

As I walked through the hotel lobby, I ran into the film crew.

"Hello, I'm Jim Davis, Producer of WSTI TV in New York."

"Yes, Jim, I heard you folks were here. If there's anything special you need, let me know."

"Electrical outlets. We plan on using a lot of lights and about three cameras for this film."

"Okay, I'll check with maintenance and get it set up for you."

"We appreciate that. This is our last shoot, so it's gotta go just right. We're short on film, and we have an early flight to New York tomorrow."

"Don't worry, Jim. You just shoot and we'll do the rest."

It was a Friday night, busier than the rest of the week, for this was the night many locals were out dancing. Already a small crowd had started to gather by the lounge entrance.

"Barefoot, Barefoot, good to see you."

It was Sam, a close friend. Sam was one of the first locals I had become friends with on my arrival to the island.

"Sam, good to see you. What are you celebrating? I haven't seen you out in ages."

"Tonight it's my anniversary...fifteen years, so play something special for me later so I can shake a leg."

I didn't see Sam's wife, so I just figured she was in the powder room.

In the lounge, table candles were lit, and waitresses were cursing in obscene island mumbo-jumbo at their latest expatriate bar manager who was not present. I turned on the tape deck, and the blaring-bassy Bob Marley reggae never even stirred a sleeping security guard sitting only a few feet from the four foot speaker box. The doorman hadn't shown up yet, so the night manager opened the gate and started taking cover-charge money.

I saw Sam grab a table close to the dance floor. By his side sat an attractive dark-skinned lady at least twenty years younger than he. I knew Sam's wife...and that wasn't her.

"Don't forget my song, Barefoot," shouted Sam.

"No way, old friend," I responded.

I guessed his wife was still in the powder room.

Another security guard walked in, woke the sleeping one and said..."Listen, mohn, you go take your break now...I take over."

By now, it was about 8:45. The balance of the band started trickling in, the drummer, the keyboard man...and finally...Harry.

"Harry, guess what? You're gonna be in the movies."

"Da movie...in a flim?" responded Harry.

"Well, actually television...so do an extra good limbo show tonight."

"You no worry, Jawg...you no worry."

By 9:30, we were halfway into our first set, and the room was nearly filled. The mixture of the crowd was, as always, 75% tourists listening for the double-meaning words in an average calypso.

SO I GIVE THE LADY A COCONUT,
SHE SAY I LIKE IT...IT OK BUT,
THEN SHE GAVE IT BACK TO ME,
WHAT GOOD ARE DA NUTS,
WITHOUT DA TREE.

The other 25% of the crowd were the locals. Now these fall into two categories:

1. The Land Sharks...these guys are there six nights a week from the time we open the gates until closing (unless they get lucky). They're not groupies; in fact most of them criticize and put down our type of music...they are regulars because they're hunting fresh white meat. And since our band attracts the tourists...we also attract the land sharks.

Now please, if you're thinking that reads like a very racist statement...it's not meant to be, for land sharks come in all varieties. There are great whites, black tips, and hammerheads. The hammerheads are the worst; they hammer away at some poor unwilling-to-dance tourist until she finally gives in...then after one calypso they do a transformation...the shark becomes a leach.

2. Then there are the locals who just love to calypso, murangee, soca and cha-cha. Since very few bands still produce this type of sound, we get our share of fun-loving islanders who want to rent-a-tile (claim a small section of the dance floor for an entire evening). And of course there are the islanders celebrating a special occasion...

"What about my anniversary song?" shouted Sam.

"Haven't forgotten you, Sam...be patient," I said into the microphone.

During an instrumental version of "Yellow Bird," I scanned the smokey, noisy, lounge...but Sam's wife was not around. She can't still be in the powder room, I thought.

Around 10:00 p.m. we took our first intermission, and Sam approached the stage. "Hey, Barefoot...I thought you were my friend."

"Sam, why would you think any different?"

"My song...It's my anniversary...did you forget?"

"No, Sam...I was just waiting for your wife so you two could dance together."

"My wife, she's at home...I got my woman here tonight. Come on, play da tune, mohn."

Before we started our second set, I made an announcement:

"Ladies and gentlemen, I'm sure you've noticed the floodlights...and camera crew. Tonight we are filming a segment for the weekly TV show...THOSE AMAZING ANIMALS...and you are the stars."

My audience rewarded me with a few laughs so I tried another shot at being a comedian: "This will be on national television in a few weeks, so before we start filming, those of you vacationing in the tropics with someone you're not supposed to be vacationing with...might want to leave the room."

With that the laughter multiplied...but the audience was reduced by several uneasy couples. (It was meant to be a joke.)

During the second set...I dedicated a special slow rub-a-baggie tune (very slow body-grinding music) to Sam and his wife Elluamay. Sam, dancing shamelessly with his date, gave me the thumbs-up every time he turned in our direction.

I reminded the audience about the limbo show and we took our second intermission for the evening. The TV producer, very happy with the filming so far, now added extra spotlights, cameras and wires to the already confusing technical mess.

By now the room was crammed to capacity. The cigarette smoke, smell of beer and rum, combined with the sounds of chatter, laughter and clinking of glass spawned a classic nightclub atmosphere that's second home to us lounge musicians.

The house lights were dimmed...and I introduced Harry...

"Okay folks...let's put our hands together...here he is, Harry-the-limbo-dancer."

The cheering crowd started to congest around the dance floor for a better look. The camera crews' blinding spots were turned on as Harry leapt ballerina-style onto the dance floor. We got a big kick out of Harry's over-enthusiastic reaction to the lights and cameras. Normally his entrance was no more than a slow paced walk.

Bending backwards, he went under the limbo pole for the first round...then lower...and then even lower...There are six nails on two poles holding up the limbo stick...halfway through his act Harry sets the limbo stick on fire. This is usually done by squirting a few shots of lighter fluid along the length of the stick...then igniting it with flames from a torch held between his teeth. This night, however, with cameras rolling, Harry added a few extra splashes (almost half a can of fluid). Well...I had told him to put on an extra special show this night.

Harry bent like a bow, and the audience screamed with excitement. The flame of the torch made contact with the fluid-saturated stick and "POOF," there was a miniature explosion...Harry's mustache, along with the end of his nose, were singed, as black smoke filled the already reeking room. The crowd loved it...they thought it was part of the act. Of course...we loved it, too. Harry's big chance to make national TV almost went up in smoke. Being a good showman...he continued, hiding his blunder with extra dance steps, giving the fire time to smolder.

As Harry went under the very last nail (about 12 inches off the floor) his fans were clapping and foot-stomping in time with the music...HE DID IT...he went under the last nail...the mob roared with approval...

"More...more."

"Alright, Harry...that was great."

"Encore...Encore."

Harry radiated from all the cheering...so he gave his audience more.

He got two empty beer bottles, placed them on the floor and balanced the limbo stick on the mouth of each bottle. This had the crowd going wild...they couldn't believe this was possible. We increased the tempo of the music, and the pleased TV producer ordered cameramen to move in for a closer shot. This was going to be some great footage.

Harry folded his muscular legs like a jack-knife...and worm-like inched his way under the stick, now only half a foot off the floor. He was almost through with the grand finale, his back flat against the polished dance floor, his exhaled chest grazing the stick...that's when it happened.

From the congested crowd, a young, attractive, slender, well-tanned blond wearing a very short sundress joined in the act. First she danced around Harry several times, then, she squatted on Harry's already burnt nose. The crowd went wild and Harry's body went rigor mortis stiff, except for one foot doing a slight vibration. As her encore...she lifted her dress for the cameras...then turned to a half-shocked, half-approving audience, giving them all a sample of what Harry had just sampled. (By the way...she wasn't tanned all over.)

As fast as she appeared...she disappeared back into the crowd.

And so ended another night of performing on a tropical island. The television crew obviously couldn't use the now x-rated footage...The mystery lady was never seen again ...and Harry was the envy of every land shark on the island.

"WHERE'S TOM JONES?"

Las Vegas—oh, what an exciting town. The lights, the shows, the stars, the money, the whole mood of the city electrifies me. (I can only take it for a few days.) Now, I'm really straying away from tropical shores again; however, I've saved the best "Harry story" for last. This is an encore in more ways than one. When I was fired from my first singing job in the Virgin Islands, I never thought for a second that one day I'd be performing in Las Vegas. After all, that is the top of the line gig for any performer. Why, just to say, "Oh yeah, I've played Vegas" seems to exude a bit of clout around most musicians.

"We're going to Las Vegas next month," I said to my drummer.

"M-MMM, where's that?" he asked.

"Las Vegas...Las Vegas...Nevada...every superstar in the world performs there," I said, bubbling over.

"MMM...good," he responded without the slightest trace of excitement.

The keyboard player's reaction was about the same. But Harry... "Wha...?, Las Vegas? Wha...dat good, Jawg; I gon win plenty dis time. You see."

Harry and I had often been to Vegas (strictly as tourists); and with every trip, he returned full of new ideas on how he will break the casinos. Once he had a well-planned strategy worked out...he and his girlfriend started with $500.00. They were playing roulette. He would put ten dollars on red, and she put ten on black; so one of the two won ten dollars with every spin of the wheel. Harry was very proud of his scheme.

"You see, Jawg, one of us always win."

"Sure, Harry, but one of you always loses, too," I said, confused at his theory.

"NO—NO, Jawg, watch..."

The wheel spun round...the ball landed on red...and a ten dollar chip was added to Harry's stack. "You see, Jawg...you see..."

"But, Harry, your friend is playing with your money, and she just lost ten dollars..." (Harry never heard a word I said.)

"Jawg, Jawg...you no understan'...watch dis time."

Harry, so sure of his scheme, put down $200.00, and his girl friend did the same on the opposite color.

The croupier advised the pit boss of the bet, spun the wheel...and Harry confidently adjusted his gold cufflinks. His girl friend bounced up and down, shrieking as the ball ricocheted from black to red, onto another red, into the black, and then made a final stop on "OO"...GREEN. I disappeared into the crowded casino, leaving a bewildered Harry and girl friend counting their last $100.00.

On this visit, we were booked to play at the Riviera Hotel for what is known as the DEMA convention. (DIVING EQUIPMENT MANUFACTURERS ASSOCIATION)

I knew those silly scuba-songs would pay off one day.

> THEY CALL HIM JEFF THE MUFF-DIVER,
> HE'S A REAL CONNIVER
> HE'S THE ONE TO ME...WHO'S MADE DIVING
>   HISTORY
> JEFF...THE MUFF-DIVER

It was the evening before we were to leave for Vegas. The band and I were packed and ready, especially Harry. He was collecting quarters for the slots and giving us a run-down on all the stars he'd seen performing in Vegas.

"Tom Jones...wha, him good you know," said Harry.

"You've seen him live?" asked Duane, the bartender.

"'Im...I see 'im, Wayne Newton, an' Paula Anka, too," said Harry proudly.

"Gee, as often as you've been to Las Vegas, how come you haven't been discovered yet?" asked the drummer jokingly.

"You guys make too much joke, mohn...one day you be sarry," responded Harry.

Their poking fun at Harry inspired me to do something really low and wicked. I left the jesting group and went into the hotel's reservations office. There I turned on the telex machine and typed a message:

> TO HARRY
> C/O BAREFOOT MAN AND BAND
>   RIVIERA HOTEL
>   LAS VEGAS

HARRY, I HEARD YOU WERE IN TOWN.
COULD YOU HELP ME OUT? MY BASS
PLAYER IS VERY SICK. I NEED A REPLACE-
MENT FOR A FEW NIGHTS.

TOM JONES, THE MGM HOTEL
LAS VEGAS, NV

For good measure, I added a few fictional
codes...LVG-679000-83code 27005-34.

I had this printed out and stashed away in my briefcase.
I know; I'm rotten. Yes, it was a dirty trick, but I couldn't
resist. Now, all that was needed was the right time and place
to put the trick into action.

Our flight arrived in Vegas about one hour late. Later in
the story you'll see the importance of my mentioning this.

In a rented car, we drove down Las Vegas Boulevard to
the Riviera. By now everyone in the band, along with Duane,
was in on the joke. (The bartender followed us to Vegas).
The plan was to check into the hotel and, sometime that
evening when we knew Harry was definitely in his room,
give a bellman a nice tip to deliver the message.

We had to stop for a red light...right next to the MGM
Hotel. That's when I figured my whole dirty scheme was
defused. There on the giant marquee it read:

TONIGHT...TONY ORLANDO
DON'T MISS OUR $2,000,000 JACKPOT

"Damn," I thought to myself, "it would have been a great
joke."

"Der, look, mohn, Caesar Palace. Dat da place dey 'ave
big fight," exclaimed Harry.

"Wow...look at all the lights. Diana Ross is there tonight.

Look, Harry, look...look," said Duane.

"Me see, me see, mohn."

Duane continued, "Look, Harry, look at the water fountain."

"Me know, mohn...me been 'ere plenty."

I picked up immediately what Duane was up to. By keeping everyone's attention on the other side of the street, he hoped Harry would not notice TONY ORLANDO on the MGM marquee.

He had to have seen it, I thought to myself, *unless he's completely blind. The MGM marquee must be the largest on the Vegas strip. And the letters, why they must be 10 feet high. He saw it, I'm sure of it.*

Our bags, guitars, and boxes were spread around the Riviera's lobby. While I was taking care of the checking in business, Harry and the crew dashed for the adjoining casino. I got room keys, coupons for a $1.99 breakfast, and a RIVIERA HOTEL envelope. Inside the envelope, I placed Harry's bogus telegram from Tom Jones. What da hell, I thought, maybe he missed the marquee.

"Let's go, guys," I shouted across the lobby. "I've got our rooms. Let's freshen up a bit, have dinner, see a show, and hit the other casinos."

"Jawg, look, mohn. Me win twenty dalla' awredy," said Harry.

"Great, Harry, great..." I responded.

"I just lost twenty," said Duane.

Henry and Jimmy (two other members of the band at that time) had yet to be infected with the gambling fever. As we waited for a slow elevator to make its way to the lobby floor, I passed Harry the envelope.

"Wha' dis is?" he queried.

"I have no idea, Harry. It was waiting for you at the front desk," was my straight-faced response.

Harry opened the envelope that had his name neatly typed on it. (A pleasant young lady working behind the front desk did this for me.) He read the message, then looked again at his name on the envelope, his mouth opening to the same circumference of his now widened eyes, and then he went berserk.

"Jawg, mohn...LOOK...LOOK...TOM JONES!!!"

Duane, Henry, Jimmy and I did a fast scan of the lobby.

"Where, Harry?" I said. "I don't see Tom Jones."

"'ere mohn, 'ere. Look at dis." Harry paced in a small circle and handed me his message. I read it, putting on a great act of surprise.

"Well, Jawg, wha' you dink?"

"Harry, I don't know what to say. It must be some kind of joke."

"JOKE....JOKE? Dis no jest, mohn. Look. Read (he jerked the message out of my hand). Tom Jones, MGM 'otel. Dat wha' it sa."

"That's what it says alright," confirmed Duane, reading the counterfeit telex.

"Jawg, you jealous, you jealous, mohn," barked Harry as his circular pacing increased.

Jimmy agreed with Harry that the note looked very official and authentic. Henry agreed with Harry that I was just jealous.

By now the elevator had stopped and gone several times, and it was apparent we had done a superb job stumping a very excited bass player.

"Jawg, can I go? Can I go play for Tom Jones?"

"Harry, you are your own man. I can't stop you, but don't forget we have a commitment to do a show tomorrow night."

"No problem, Jawg. I explain to Tom."

Harry grabbed his bass guitar and rushed for the door. A few minutes later he reappeared, almost catching our mischievous, guilty snickering.

"Jawg, mohn, you go wit me...I not know wha' to do."

"First thing, Harry, calm down a bit. Next, have the cab driver take you down the back street, direct to the stage entrance (this would also keep Harry away from the marquee). If any security try to stop you, just show them your telex. If that doesn't work, demand to see Tom Jones."

"Good idea, Jawg, good idea."

We waved goodbye and shouted "good luck" as he sped away in the first available cab.

Now what happened after this? We could only leave it to our imagination.

Did he finally see the giant marquee advertising Tony Orlando and catch on to our jest? Did he go to the stage door and present his letter? Did the manager of the MGM Hotel have him booted out? Was he carried away in a straight jacket? We'd never know.

But one thing we did know; he'd never get out of this one.

In the hotel lobby we anxiously waited for his return, rehearsing the tormenting remarks we'd planned for him. Nearly an hour passed and no sign of Harry.

"Maybe he's in jail," said Duane.

"He's probably out buying a gun to blow us all away," said Henry.

Jimmy pointed to the revolving door, "There he is!"

And there he was. As he walked toward us, his face and his pace could only be described like that of a five-year-old child who had just witnessed his puppy dog run over by a speeding mack truck. I couldn't do it to him. I couldn't accelerate this gag by laughing now. I must admit, I felt scummy (just for a second) playing such a dirty trick on my pitiful-looking bass player.

"Harry, what happened?" said Duane, showing much concern.

"Did you see Tom Jones or what?" asked Jimmy.

"Mohn, you guys wouldn't believe wha' 'appen."

"What, Harry? What...?" I said.

"Because our flight late comin' to Vegas, dey cancel da whole damn show...an' TONY ORLANDO 'ave to play instead."

Harry left us knavish scoundrels looking at each other in amazement at his classic of classic comebacks...he did it again.

Another Harry Classic...

Me: "Harry, you forgot to turn off your instruments."

Harry: "No, Jawg. I was just about to remember."

Peopl

The
Cayman
Islands

X

My Tales Of
The South Pacific

The South Pacific...those two words mean as much to a beachcomber as "Hollywood" does to someone in search of stardom, or "Super Bowl" to a football jock.

Dreams of the South Seas have always been in my head. I pictured a place where empty beaches are plentiful, the lagoons are calm, and the people are as warm as constant sunshine.

A map of the vast Pacific Ocean shows thousands of islands scattered everywhere. Many of these are actually atolls; one atoll, like Manihiki, can be made up of 39 islands. Just the names of these sandy palm covered dots are enough to get any beachcomber excited. Bora Bora, Vanuatu, Tahiti, Samoa, Tonga...with neat sounding names like that, they make one want to build an outrigger canoe and sail into the sunset.

That's the only way to see the South Pacific—under sail. Let the wind carry you, with no smell of jet fuel or rumbling of a freighter's engine...sail away to paradise.

A few friends and I did exactly that aboard the 49-foot sailing ketch "Roscop." We sailed through Polynesia in search of the perfect island, Bora Bora. It's a long "island-hop," my friends, from the Caribbean to Bora Bora; but it represents yet another dream unfulfilled, another shore on which to leave the imprints of my feet to be washed away by incoming tides.

Alberto (the Galleon Beach Hotel Bar Manager), Pop, better known as Lord Layton Lyon, and I agreed one balmy full-mooned tropical night to share expenses in chartering the sailing vessel known as the "Roscop." Pop, a retired department store owner from Williamsport, Pennsylvania, and a regular visitor to the Caymans, was captivated with my maps and books on the South Pacific. Pop was much older than Alberto and I, sort of lanky in size, except for a big belly that almost gave him a pregnant look and the bags under his eyes—features that made him look very much like a tiki god. Being the close friend he was, we knew he would make a good companion on such a voyage.

After some arrangements with a charter company, we found the "Roscop" to be just the right size vessel for us, so this adventure-seeking trio headed for the South Seas (what the hell...it's only money). Our first stop was Tahiti; then we began a 40-minute flight to Huahine to meet our Captain and crew, consisting of Rein Mortier, his wife Louise, and two sassy cats.

Huahine (population about 4,000) does not have all the fame accorded Tahiti and Bora Bora; however, it has something very special. It's quiet, peaceful and almost untouched by the flow of tourists visiting French Polynesia.

We spent the first two rainy nights docked at Fare, Huahine's main village. Fare sort of looks like a cowboy town, sitting beside a tropical lagoon—a few Chinese shops, a small bank, and...Mama Pini's Saloon.

"Good morning, gentlemen," said a big, round, smiling, bronze-skinned lady wearing a crown of red and yellow flowers. "I Mama Pini. Can I fix you breakfast?"

"Sounds great," I answered.

Alberto, half asleep, said, "Make that two."

"Mama Pini, when will this rain ever stop?" I asked.

"Oh, but, sir, rain good. It will wash clean the land and help ripen breadfruit."

"What does this have to do with my tan?" I wondered.

A short, stout, elderly white man wearing a straw hat joined us. "Gentlemen, good morning. I overheard you speaking English...My name is Dr. John Kalseer, and this is my wife Rosa. We are from the village of Haapu. Welcome to Huahine."

"Thank you, John," we said, shaking his hand.

"Welcome to Huahine," said Rosa with a bear hug, followed by a kiss on each cheek. Rosa, like Mama Pini (or should I say like most middle-age women in the South Pacific) was very big. For some strange, mysterious reason Polynesian women are always beautiful, even when they get chunky. The warmth we encountered in the first few moments of entering Mama Pini's bar made us forget the pouring rain just outside the old wooden structure.

John was very excited to meet some English speaking visitors; this gave him a great opportunity to tell someone about his interests. He studied the language of the Polynesian people and how the language had originated. We didn't want to be rude; so through our breakfast of lobster, raw fish, rice and ripe breadfruit, we listened. Rosa brought on Hinano beer, and the rain came down in buckets as we listened...

"You see, then, the canoes sailed from Hawaii, and after that...stopped in the Marquesas Islands and..." ZZZZZZZZZZZZZZZ...Listening to John, Alberto and I fell into badly needed sleep on the bamboo bar stools. The flight from Los Angeles to Tahiti and on to Huahine had been a long one. So while John jabbered away about Polynesian etymology, we snored.
ZZZZZZZZZZZZZZZZZZZZZZZZ...

John had arrived in Tahiti as a young sailor from Amsterdam, married an island girl and moved to her village, Haapu. While the other men of the village fished and planted breadfruit, John educated himself by reading any book he could find on Polynesia. He is one of the most knowledgeable people on the South Pacific I've ever come across. However, intellectual John lives in a village comprised of islanders who couldn't care less about the origin of their native tongue. So when he found a willing audience...he never stopped..."And the people of Micronesia...they went north on to...The Hawaiian chiefs also sailed...etc.,etc.,..."
ZZZZZZZZZZZZZZZZZZZZZZZZ....

A short nap later, we woke to John's historical chitchat, Rosa's dancing and Mama Pini's singing.

The buckets of rain had now turned to a soft drizzle, and the dock area across the street became busy with islanders dressed in brightly colored cloths called "pareu". The colorful, rectangular-shaped piece of cloth is worn by men and women alike...but there in no question that the vahines (island girls) wear it best. Wrapped around their brown bodies, they seem to paint a picture of a mythical Polynesia that has changed little since the arrival of the first outsiders aboard the "HMS Dolphin" in 1767.

Today the islanders were awaiting the weekly arrival of the freighter "Taporo III." The freighter delivers goods for the Chinese shops and transports islanders between Tahiti, Raiatea, and Huahine. There are a few cabins on the "Taporo" but most people just sleep on the rusted deck, along with piglets and crates filled with noisy chickens. I've heard this is a fun way to see the more remote islands in the Pacific. The quiet dock area turned into a busy marketplace as the freighter's horn signaled its arrival. Fishermen sold strings of brightly colored fish, and Chinese vendors sold everything from sweet cakes to plates of fafaru (raw fish). Don't turn up your noses...it's good. Watermelons, breadfruit, and coconuts bordered the road area, adding yet more charm to the colorful market.

Islanders kissed and hugged each other as they boarded the old ship for its journey to Tahiti.

"Ah, there he is," shouted John.

"Who is?" asked Alberto.

"Turru, Rosa's brother from Tahiti; he's coming for a visit." John introduced Alberto and me to Turru who looked to be in his mid-40's, with more oriental features than Polynesian. He was about the height of Alberto (short). Turru smiled at us, then followed with a Polynesian embrace.

"That's a nice shirt, Turru," I said, admiring the bright red flower-coconut tree design. John translated to Turru; Turru dropped his bags and proceeded to take off his shirt.

"He wants you to have it," said John.

"No, I can't; I was just making conversation. It's a nice shirt, but I...tell him I can't."

"You best take it," said John. "It's Polynesian tradition to give. This is a tradition that goes way back to..."

Oh no, not another history lesson, I thought to myself.

A shirtless Turru grinned with approval as I accepted his gift. "Just like you to take advantage of the islanders the minute you step on their beach," said Alberto.

"Aw, come on. I was just admiring his shirt. I didn't mean for him to give it to me," I said defensively.

"Don't worry about it...buy Turru a few beers," said John. "That will make him happy."

Captain Rein and Louise were waiting by the busy dock area.

"We are ready to set sail for Bora Bora. The ship has been stocked with supplies, the rain is gone and the wind is ready to fill our sails," said the Captain.

Captain Rein couldn't have weighed more than a hundred

pounds. He was well-tanned and always wore those skimpy, tiny, body clinging bathing suits that Europeans like to wear. This attire suited his shapely, petite wife, Louise, just fine, but Rein looked much better in his pareu.

"I'm ready—Bora Bora, here we come," was my response.

"I've been ready," said Alberto. "Now we have to find Pop."

"Oh yes, George, could you please speak to your friend Pop?" said a blushing Louise.

"Why? Is there something wrong?"

"Well, he's showering on the bow of the boat...COMPLETELY NAKED! The villagers are talking. You see, we have to return to Huahine. This is our home."

"Sorry, Louise."

"You cannot sail away to Bora Bora just like that," said John with a disappointed look on his face. "You promised to visit our village. Rosa and Turru are looking forward to it."

Louise took us over to one side. "If you promised them a visit, we best go to Haapu first. It's apparent these people have taken a liking to you guys. Should you disappoint them, they would take it very seriously."

"But, Louise, when they asked us to come to their village, I only said 'yes' to be nice."

"Then be nice and keep your promise."

"Another fine mess you got us into, Ollie," said Alberto.

We motored to Haapu, staying inside the reef all the way. We were happy about our decision to stay a while; Hauhine is certainly a lovely island.

Huahine is in fact two islands, Huahine-Nui and Huahine-Iti. Both islands lie in the same lagoon, surrounded by the same barrier reef. A bridge connects the two islands, and at a low tide you can walk from island to island without use of the bridge. The two islands are made up of several high green mountains, and white sandy beaches are scattered all along the coastline.

We passed islanders fishing in their outriggers, and they waved as if greeting long lost friends.

As the sun set on our first day aboard the "Roscop," we anchored in a quiet bay just off Haapu. The five of us sat in the galley, sang songs and drank margaritas. Between the mixing of tequila and lime, our Belgian hosts told us about their sail around the world and how they finally settled in Huahine. Part of the year, they charter, and the rest of the time Captain Rein paints; he is a fine artist. (Note his art work in this book.)

The tale of their voyage was interrupted by Pop's praying. "Oh, thank you, tiki. Thank you for bringing us to these beautiful islands...Thank you for the company of Rein and Louise...Thank you for...

"Who's that he's talking to?" I asked Rein.

"Tangaroa."

"Tanga...what?"

"Tangaroa...the carved tiki."

In the center of the small galley dining table was a carved wooden tiki about two feet high, and Pop was in deep devotions rubbing the tiki's head as he spoke.

"And thank you for the rain that has ripened the breadfruit...and for this drink I am about to receive."

With that he fixed another cocktail.

The Captain and Louise passed out fast; trying to keep up with Layton's and Alberto's consumption of tequila was too much for them (or anyone). I went up top, and like a hibernating bear, curled up in a lowered sail. Distant singing from Haapu lullabied me to sleep.

The following morning, we had a breakfast of pineapple and French bread, then via rubber dinghy, headed towards shore. There was John waiting for us with a crowd of young inquisitive children. "Welcome to Haapu, my friends. Rosa is preparing a breakfast of pineapple and French bread."

We looked at each other...but said nothing. John embraced everyone, then invited us on a village tour before proceeding to his home. The beautiful brown-skinned children followed us, dancing in the muddy street.

"Come. We must stop by the home of the village chief; he is expecting us," said John.

I envisioned a big Tahitian, sitting on a throne made of bamboo, surrounded by topless island girls. The chief of the town council greeted us with wine, french bread and pineapple. He was a small fellow, wearing checkered shorts and a tank top T-shirt advertising Hinano Beer. Like everyone else, a big smile was plastered on his face. On the front porch of his cinder block home, we ate and drank wine while John translated for us endless questions from the chief. During this time, children peeked around every corner of the small house.

"John, are all these his children?" I asked.

"Yes, all twelve of them."

The chief nodded; he seemed to know what we were talking about.

"They are beautiful...John, tell the chief I said his children are beautiful."

John translated my message, and the chief's smile widened from ear to ear.

"No-No, chief," said John.

The chief nodded in a yes-yes motion.

"No, no, Chief," followed by a lot of island dialogue.

"What's going on John?" I asked.

Before John had a chance to answer, the chief shouted out an order to all the children; they then disappeared into their home.

"Did I say something wrong, John?"

"Quite the contrary, my friend. The chief is honored that you gentlemen admire his children. It's just that...well, I don't know how to explain..."

"What is it, John?"

"You'll see," he said, adding a mysterious grin.

The chief picked up an old out-of-tune guitar and sang, while his chunky wife brought on more food. Several tunes later, she returned, having changed into a colorful flowered loose dress. She interrupted the music with a whisper in the chief's ear. The chief stood up and went into a long abstract speech, with a very obvious proud look on his face. Then, one at a time, his children returned, this time only the girls, each wearing a different colored pareu, their long black hair neatly combed, with a flower placed behind one ear.

They lined up in front of us. My first guess is that their ages ranged from ten to twenty. They smiled at us as the chief again spoke in a language foreign to our ears.

"The Chief is telling you the names of his children," said John.

"Wow, isn't this something," I whispered to Alberto and Layton.

"It's too much; this is only supposed to happen to Marlon Brando in MUTINY ON THE BOUNTY," said Captain Rein.

John continued translating...

"George, the chief asks if you fellows would like to take one of his daughters."

"WHAT? TAKE ONE OF HIS WHAT??"

Pop just grinned with a wide-eyed dirty-old-man look, Alberto sat there pinching himself, and I stammered and stuttered...not knowing exactly what to say.

"The Polynesian people have a tradition of giving, and you told the chief his children were beautiful; now he wants to know if you would like one of his daughters."

"John, I was just admiring their beauty. I was just trying

to be nice to the chief. Make friendly conversation...he can't be serious."

"He could be serious, but not in the western world-fashion of a one-night stand...he means take one for good."

"John, tell the chief we appreciate his kind offer; however this would be one souvenir we could never explain to our wives."

"Oh, thank you, tiki god...THANK YOU...My wife wouldn't mind," said Pop.

"Oh hush-up, Pop. We better get out of this village before we end up in a cooking pot."

Alberto agreed. That is what movie scripts are made of, and we weren't ready to be sacrificed. After about three more meals at different homes and a visit with John's family, we made our slow departure out of Bourayne Bay (minus the chief's daughters). Children, John, Rosa, Turru, and the chief waved a farewell from the palm fringed shores of Huahine.

The fragrance from flowers around my neck, mixed with the salty fresh smell of the ocean, spun me in sort of a daydreaming trance.

Words came to mind that were published in the *London Chronicle* in 1768, just after the "HMS Dolphin" returned from her voyage to the South Seas:

"WE HAVE DISCOVERED A LARGE, FERTILE, EXTREMELY POPULOUS ISLAND IN THE SOUTH SEAS...'TIS IMPOSSIBLE TO DESCRIBE THE BEAUTIFUL PROSPECTS WE BEHELD IN THIS CHARMING SPOT..."

While Pop again spoke to the tiki, Louise prepared a dinner of steamed fish, rice, and banana pudding in her small galley. Captain Rein held firm to his ship's wheel, as the wind filled every inch of the giant canvas moving us steadily towards

Raiatea. Raiatea is the largest of the Polynesian leeward islands, and also the administrative center for this area. Its capitol, Uturoa, is no big metropolis; but it does have a hospital, three banks, a courthouse, boutiques, a pharmacy, and several shops that sell parts for outboard engines.

The Captain needed a few spark plugs and some other odds and ends, so we planned a fast stop in Uturoa before continuing on to Bora Bora. Our happy hour conversation sailing away from Huahine centered, of course, on "The Chief" and his many children.

"Captain, do you think he was really serious about giving away his daughters?" asked Layton.

"I'm not sure. I've lived in Huahine for several years, and that's the first time I've ever witnessed such a thing."

"It had to be a joke," said Alberto.

"Ya, I agree...Maybe John doesn't understand Polynesian as well as he thinks," I said.

"Well, as I say, I'm not sure. The Polynesian families are very close, so that makes me doubt that he was serious; but then again, they are strong in traditions, and they seem to have taken a liking to you three...I cannot understand why," added the Captain humorously.

"Captain, we're not fussy, nor do we have any intentions of discrediting these people by placing ourselves in a class better than them. I believe they sensed that. We ate with them, we sang with them, laughed with them, and...we didn't throw pennies in the lagoon, expecting a retrieval."

The Captain agreed. If anyone could appreciate what I was saying it was Rein and Louise. They had actually been adopted by a Polynesian family.

"Yes, my friends, there is lots of love in Huahine. Just look at her," said Rein as he pointed off stern. "Tell me, what do you see?"

Watching the island disappear behind us, Alberto was

the first to notice..."It's a woman...A PREGNANT WOMAN."

"That's right," said Rein.

I looked at the distant green islands for some time, then I, too, saw it. The mountains of Huahine formed a giant expectant figure laying on her back, in the blue rolling Pacific.

Before we indulged ourselves in the tasty looking spread prepared for us, again Pop spoke to the tiki...

"Thank you...thank you...I'm so honored to be here with you. Thank you for the wonderful food we are about to receive...bless the Chief and his lovely daughters..."

"You know something, Alberto, he's starting to look like that tiki," I whispered.

Alberto agreed. Pop, with his bulging belly and always sleepy-looking eyes, bore a strong resemblance to the tiki on the table.

The following day, the Captain did his errands and Louise gave us a first class tour of Uturoa's busy little market. No doubt about it; this is the island meeting spot. Or should I say "gossip spot"? It's easy to lip read idle rumor, even if you do not understand the native tongue. Between chatter, islanders sold watermelons, mangos, and fresh fish. Pawpaw and sacks of copra made great resting spots for the merchants. Other stalls in the market displayed hats, carved tikis, mother-of-pearl shells, and a large assortment of wooden carved bowls and cups.

We stopped at one of the stalls and ate firi-firi, sort of a local doughnut, and then hopped aboard a "truck" (the local bus) for a more expanded look at Raiatea. Close to 7,000 people live on this fertile island that shares its surrounding reef with the smaller island Tahaa. We sandwiched ourselves between islanders, produce, and fish as the driver of the "truck" stopped every several hundred yards, letting passengers off or on.

My thoughts again went back to pages of history I've read

on these islands.

Raiatea was the home of Omai. On Captain Cook's second voyage to the South Seas, Omai persuaded Cook to take him back to England; thus, he became the first Polynesian to visit London. Omai became a popular figure in English high society, dining in some of London's finest homes and becoming a hit with the ladies. He even met King George and was said to have said, "How do, King Tosh?" This must have turned up many snobbish British noses.

However, King George liked the well-mannered Omai and even gave him an allowance and a sword. A few years after his arrival, the King ordered Cook to take Omai back. Why??...I guess we'll never know. But, I believe Omai's popularity with the ladies may have been the reason for his deportation. After all, I'm sure it must have been some novelty for the high society females to be held by a real-live muscular savage instead of the graceful hankie-holding lords and earls.

As Omai departed for Tahiti in 1776, a good portion of the ship's cargo was an accumulation of gifts from his many female admirers, including muskets, pistols, globes, wines, and outrageous clothes he could never wear in tropical Polynesia. Back in Tahiti, Omai was once again a second class citizen. The islanders were not impressed with his fancy attire or his stories of dining with lords and ladies. In fact, the island chiefs resented the idea that he had been given gifts of greater value than theirs.

Omai became sort of an outcast; so Cook took him to Hauhine where he built him a home to store all his presents. Before Cook's crew departed, they finished off his wine. It was not too long after that that Omai died, and all his souvenirs vanished.

"Bali Hai, this Bali Hai," shouted the driver, bringing me

out of my Omai daydream.

Since we were the only tourist-looking types aboard his bus, the driver figured that was our stop. The Bali Hai of Raiatea is a first class hotel built amongst the island's lush surroundings. This resort was not on our itinerary, but the "what-are-you-waiting-for" stares from other passengers made us depart. There we had a few VERY expensive cocktails, while watching beautiful vahines perform the Hula for hotel guests.

Our unexpected stop brought us back to the "Roscop" later than planned, so our Captain suggested we motor towards Tahaa instead of making the sail to Bora Bora at night.

"I know a perfect little motu (island). We can anchor there tonight, and after breakfast tomorrow, we sail for Bora Bora," proposed Rein.

We all agreed, untied the ropes; and a few hours later, as sunset turned the sky into a brilliant bright orange, we dropped anchor off a small island smothered with tall coconut trees.

"Hey, wake up," shouted Alberto, passing a cup of hot coffee my way. "You're not going to believe this place; this is truly paradise."

"What? Are we in Bora Bora already?"

"No we're still anchored off the little island. Get up! You've slept half the morning."

The morning sun spotlighted the tiny island in all its glorious, palm fringed splendor. It could not have been more than a mile long, and maybe a few hundred yards wide. The transparency of the water almost gave the island a floating-on-air effect.

The only ripple in the glassy water was caused by Pop's routine morning swim. If the sight of this little paradise hadn't been enough to quench my thirst for tropical islands, tranquil-looking Tahaa on our starboard side did me in.

I dove in the calm lagoon and swam towards the miniature Eden. Alberto, Rein, Louise and Pop followed close behind. We sat on the small beach, admiring Mother Nature's stunning spectacle.

"Captain, if it's okay with you and everyone else, I'd like to stay here for a while," I said.

"You mean cancel Bora Bora?" asked the Captain.

"Oh no; let's just not go today, tomorrow, or days after."

"But there's nothing here except coconut trees. No gift shops or discos...nothing!"

"Perfect," I said...and everyone else agreed.

The coral garden at the northern end of the motu offered a bountiful supply of fish and a rainbow-colored assortment of coral. We speared fish for dinner, then took a dinghy ride across the lagoon to Tahaa. There we went in search of fresh water shrimp to add to that evening's buffet. Tahaa and Raiatea share the same barrier reef. Tahaa is the smaller of the two islands, with a population of around 3,500 happy, beautiful natives. In the clear mountain streams, playing children kept us company as we filled several buckets with shrimp. The grown-ups would not let us leave without a lunch of roasted moray eel and baked breadfruit. The welcoming smiles again had us in awe. When we complimented the islanders on the taste of breadfruit, we were given a dozen to take back with us, along with necklaces made of shells.

Four days after our unplanned anchorage between Tahaa and the unnamed motu, we raised the sails and set course for what James Michener described as "the most beautiful island in the world, Bora Bora."

"Captain, is it as beautiful as they say?" asked Layton.

"It's more beautiful than they say; words cannot describe Bora Bora."

"I don't see how anything can be better than where we just spent the last four days," I said.

"Bora Bora is what dreams are made of my friends. This is where God himself vacations," said Louise.

As we entered Teavanui Pass, the deep blue Pacific exploded into a white mist upon the reef surrounding God's playground. Green Mt. Otemanu, piercing just over 2,000 feet into a cloudless blue sky, looked as striking as I had imagined it to be. Motus surround the island in all directions; and upon entering the pass, the deep dark blue water became a mixture of aqua, emerald, and blinding turquoise.

In typical tourist fashion, our cameras snapped wildly as Bora Bora's majestic beauty filled our sights. I could see why more has been written about this Eden than any other spot in the South Pacific.

You can easily ride around Bora Bora (by bicycle) in less than six hours (this includes several beer stops). There's a two-lane road that runs 32 kilometers around the island, with the lagoon on one side and steep green terrain on the other.

One thing I noticed almost instantly: the warmth, the hugs, and guaranteed smiles were not as abundant here as in Huahine and Tahaa. This Eden has been invaded by tourists, who stay in such places as Club Med, Hotel Bora Bora, and soon to come, a Hyatt (according to rumor). If this isn't enough, Italian filmmakers invaded the island to film the movie "Hurricane" in 1977.

WW II had brought the visit of some 6,000 American soldiers; however, the worst invasion of all took place in the early 1800's, when the so-called "good news" missionaries made their way to these shores and other surrounding islands. The missionaries banned traditional singing, dancing, games and lovemaking. Penalties of imprisonment were handed out to the islanders who did not obey their white "good news" invaders. Under these puritanical conditions, the happy islanders soon lost their love for life, the birth rate fell alarmingly and, by the early part of the nineteenth century, it was feared the race would be lost all together.

Because of my interest and fascination with the South Seas, I've read numerous books on its history and people. Stories of the missionaries, with their hypocritical teachings, have always put a damper on what should have been continuous reading about happy, joyful times.

Why would God have NOT wanted these contented people to sing, dance, and go naked?? I know what the "good news" missionaries would have said..."The Lord works in mysterious ways."

Pop was also starting to work in mysterious ways, spending more and more time talking to the tiki as he gently stroked its head.

"Thank you, my friend...thank you for bringing us safely to this lovely island...thank you for..."

"Hey, Pop, leave the tiki already, come on up...let's go explore a bit," I shouted through a porthole.

"Go on, I'll catch up later; he's telling me something right now."

I peeked through the porthole; and for an instant, Pop's similarity to the tiki seemed spooky.

"Too much sun," I thought. ..."I'm getting too much sun."

Near the Bora Bora Yacht club, I talked an islander into loaning me his outrigger so I could paddle to one of the many outlying islands. I must have been some sight to the skilled canoers I passed along the way. With every paddle to move right, I went left; and just as the outrigger made a slight direction to move forward, the tide would pull the bow one way and the breeze would carry the stern another. It looks so easy in the movies.

I explored a small, uninhabited island, walking on a trail of coconut fronds. The walk to the next motu was just a few steps through a clear tidal pool.

As I opened a fresh green coconut for a drink, the seclusion made me feel like the only living being on earth. Bora Bora's enticing beauty invaded my very soul. And the color scheme of the lagoon, with its shimmering blues and purples...it was all toooo...much. I walked along the beach, hearing only the sound of birds playing above and the popping-cracking sounds of tiny shells beneath my bare feet.

Our week's stay in Bora Bora was enchanting and as fulfilling as any island adventure should be. We played in the lagoon, explored the lush interior, visited the ancient temples called "marae", and even exchanged plastic beads for tropical drinks at Club Med.

On our final night before sailing back to Huahine, we treated the Captain and Louise to dinner at Bloody Mary's Restaurant. This is a spot that's a must for anyone visiting Bora Bora, even if you just use the bathroom. The restroom is on a raised platform, crowned by a toilet...exposing everything above your shoulders to surrounding flowers, trees, and birds.

The owner, an ex-airline pilot, took any piece of driftwood, bamboo log, old ship's rope, and coconut tree stumps found along the beach and built himself the most popular eating and drinking spot on the island. Fresh wiggling lobsters and fish are displayed on a large table covered with green banana leaves and wild flowers. We picked what we wanted, and it was prepared for us. Only Tarzan and Jane have enjoyed dining in such a tropical atmosphere.

With our bellies full and spirits high, we were filled with a bit of sadness, for we realized soon the voyage would come to an end. The island band starting a contagious, happy melody erased the moment of depression. We clapped along and hummed along; I was passed a guitar...so I strummed along. The house musicians sat on stools made of short tree stumps twisted into the sandy floor of the restaurant. There was an empty stool next to the ukulele player...Pop, full of island rum, somehow managed to occupy it—but only for a few seconds.

When he fell, so did the ukulele player, and the spoon player, and the bongo player. In domino fashion, the band came crashing down.

A few moments later, we found ourselves outside of Bloody Mary's in convulsive hysterical laughter, repeating the story of Pop's blunder that had gotten us kicked out of Bora Bora's most popular eating and drinking establishment.

We had a choice: to walk up the road and continue our farewell party at the classy-plush Bora Bora Hotel or to celebrate aboard the "Roscop." Fortunately for the Bora Bora Hotel...we did the latter.

Leisurely we sailed back to Huahine, stopping at more uninhabited islands along the way.

The voyage was almost at an end. I knew I would certainly miss our hosts and all the wonderful people of French Polynesia. But as I listened to Pop talk to the tiki on our final night aboard the "Roscop" I wasn't sure if he could handle his parting.

"Mah-rhu-rhu...Mah-rhu-rhu-...Mahn-wee-ah..." said Pop.
"Nah-nah...GOODBYE MY FRIENDS," said somebody.

IT WAS ME, ALBERTO AND POP
SAILING ON THE "ROSCOP"
SOMEWHERE BETWEEN BORA BORA AND TAHITI
LOUISE AND CAPTAIN REIN
WILL NEVER BE THE SAME

DRINKING HINANO BEER AT MAMA PINI'S

ON MONDAY WE PLAYED IN THE SAND
ON TUESDAY WE SANG WITH THE BAND
ON WEDNESDAY WE HOISTED SAILS
ON THURSDAY WE SAW THE WHALES
ON FRIDAY WE FELT NO PAIN
ON SATURDAY DANCED IN THE RAIN
AND ON SUNDAY...WE STARTED ALL OVER
AGAIN...

From the Song ME ALBERTO AND POP

LAGOONS, PEARLS, and MR. NEALE—
A VISIT TO THE COOK ISLANDS

French Polynesia has its share of publicity. Ask someone, "Where's Tahiti?" and even your average geography-failing high school student will know it's in the South Pacific. The French Government's nuclear testing, MUTINY ON THE BOUNTY and a lot of tourism promotion money is credited for this.

Now ask someone about The Cook Islands. Nine out of ten people have no idea where this paradise is hidden.

The fifteen Cook Islands are scattered about 751,000 square miles between Tahiti and Fiji. The main island, Rarotonga, is a formation of volcanoes where streams run from the interior to outlying lagoons. The island is surrounded by a barrier reef and, in many ways, favors Tahiti.

The Northern Cook Islands are low lying atolls. A bird's eye view of an atoll would look something like a giant necklace of jade, in the midst of a blue ocean.

Atolls are made up of numerous small, sandy, green

islands surrounding a calm lagoon; the reef connects each island like a chain made of coral.

Tom Neale's book, AN ISLAND TO ONESELF (one of my most treasured possessions), is the main reason why the Cooks have always appealed to me. Tom's stories of life alone on Suwarrow Atoll left an empty space in my wanderlust that I was determined to fill. You've not experienced the ultimate, supreme beachcomber's heaven until you've visited an atoll like Suwarrow.

Suwarrow's position in the Pacific is NNW 13°14'40" S. Now if this seems confusing...don't feel bad...I have no idea what all that means...except, in simpler terms, it's in the middle of nowhere. To get to Suwarrow you need to go 513 miles north of Rarotonga into the middle of an almost endless Pacific Ocean. There are no scheduled ships, planes, trains, or balloons that visit Suwarrow. Even coconut freighters have no reason to stop there.

Yet, with its lonely isolation, New Zealander Tom Neale made it his home for nearly 20 years, living by himself in total contentment until the late 1970's when he passed away. Tom was the unquestionable "king" of beachcombers. Trying to track down a willing captain, crew and ship to visit Suwarrow is nearly as difficult as finding navigational charts of the atoll. But, with the help of Mary Crawley, the head of Ocean Voyages in Sausalito, California, we booked the 78-foot ketch "Stormvogel". Mary's chartering company acts as sort of a travel agent for island seekers who have no interest in the group package tour-guided type of holiday. The "Stormvogel's" captain was willing to re-route his world voyage for a cruise through the Northern Cooks.

Dave (ex-Galleon Hotel Manager) and Frank, a Canadian record producer friend, and I spent a year planning our trip. We scheduled it to begin in Los Angeles, where we'd fly to Tahiti, on to Rarotonga, then to Aitutaki. Here we would

get aboard the "Stormvogel." We'd sail to Palmerston, Suwarrow, Manihiki, and Samoa. When we reached Samoa, we'd
fly to Hawaii, connecting to L.A. and back home again. The
trip would take a little over a month.

Our well planned itinerary fell apart in L.A. Frank did not
show up at our planned meeting place, and we had just 24
hours before a scheduled flight to Tahiti.

"Did you call Frank yet?" asked Dave.

"Yes, I just got through; his secretary said he had to go
to London on business, and we should go without him."

"You must be kidding, he's paid for his share of the charter,
his airline ticket, and now he's not going."

"What can I say, Dave? That's his problem...he's going
to miss the trip of a lifetime because of some record deal.
Dave, think of all that extra food and beer we'll
have...Dave...Dave..."

Dave, with a big dirty grin on his face, was lost in some
scheme. I sensed he was up to something. "What's on your
mind, Dave?"

"I've just had a great idea. Hold on, I'll be right back."

Sipping on Lite beer in the small Manhattan Beach bar,
I wondered what Dave was up to as he dialed a coin
telephone. Dave and I have been good friends for many
years. He was once my boss, during a seven-year engagement at the Galleon Beach Hotel on Grand Cayman. He
left there to take over management and part ownership of
a successful bar and restaurant operation on the same
island. Dave, about my height (short), loves looking for
adventure; and he finds it, despite his thick glasses. He
should stay out of jungles, however; with his hairy body,
he could be mistaken for an ape...and SHOT.

(two beers later)

"You'll love her, George; she's as crazy as they come."

"Who...I'll love who?" I replied.

"Ammmmm, ummmmm...What's her name? Ohhh...Joan. That's it...Joan."

"Who's Joan; who's What's Her Name?"

"Look at it like this, George. The Captain is expecting three of us, the cabins are paid for, and the food is paid for, so why not bring someone else?"

"You mean 'What's Her Name' is coming along?"

"Sure, why not? I'll buy her a ticket and champagne. She loves champagne, and..."

"Champagne...?? We're going to some of the most remote islands in the world, and she wants champagne? Dave, PLEASE...I hope you mentioned that this isn't going to be your typical weekend Caribbean cruise aboard some four hundred-foot luxury liner."

"Don't worry about it...she's crazy. You'll love her."

I was worried.

Dave's a confirmed bachelor whose taste in women finds him in the company of the more glamorous, well manicured, ritzy type of females. Now, I'm not trying to judge my friend Dave or the company he keeps; I just could not see this type of lady in the confined company of beer drinking, belching, unshaven, cursing, sweaty sailors.

With very little time to spare, "What's Her Name" arrived in Los Angeles to a greeting of Dave's hugs, kisses and roaming fingers. The winks, mixed with suspicious snickers, made me wonder if this hadn't been planned from the beginning.

Our overnight stay in Rarotonga was certainly too short. Avarua, the capital, is a small picturesque South Pacific town. The people were friendly; and the food, rooms, and Polynesian floor show at the Tamure Hotel were most pleasant and most reasonable in price.

The following day we flew on a small prop-plane north 140 miles to Aitutaki. Here we were met by our captain. A handsome Italian, Hermann looked just like a sea captain should: he was bearded, tanned, and had eyes to match the color of the sea. The "Stormvogel" was anchored outside the reef. In a rubber dinghy, Captain Hermann ferried back and forth luggage, supplies and cases of champagne...for "What's Her Name."

This took some time so I stayed on land to explore the village of Arutanga.

Children there smiled, waved, and thanked me every time I took their pictures. These people were a photographer's dream. One small boy brought me into his yard, posed with every member of his family, and, before my departing, his mother filled a coconut frond basket with pawpaws and bananas as thanks for taking their photo.

The Catholic Priest "Father George" invited me into his home, and he acted as though he'd been expecting me. His living room was decorated with shells, shark jaws, and a library of books, magazines and other reading materials.

"I'm so glad you could make it; would you care for some coffee or tea?"

"Coffee, tea...do you have a cold bee...yes, coffee please."

Along with coffee, he brought a logbook and pen. The thick book was filled with signatures and short messages:

Father George, thanks for the coffee, tea, and mangos...we loved your island, and we'll be back soon.
Capt. M.J. Thomas and Crew
"The West Wind"
Newport, R.I. USA

Your information, tea and prayer were most delightful. Thanks Father George.
The Travis Family Sailing Yacht, "Legal Aid"
Williamsport, PA   USA

As I skimmed through the interesting jottings, addresses, cartoons and silly boat names, a constantly smiling Father George brought on cookies, photo albums, and mangos. Restlessly, he moved back and forth, always checking the window for any new visitors strolling down the road.

"Did you ever meet Tom Neale?" I asked.

"Oh yes, somewhere here I have photos of him on Suwarrow."

We looked through endless volumes of photo albums; however, our search was cut short.

"Let's sail," shouted the Captain from outside.

"How did you know I was here, Captain?"

"I heard Father George captures everyone who travels down this dusty road. I'm sorry it took so long, but finding champagne for ummm...ohhh...what's her name?"

"I don't know; just call her 'What's Her Name.'"

"Anyway, finding champagne here in Aitutaki was not an easy task."

I added my name to the list of many in Father George's logbook and bid the friendly priest farewell. He promised to pray for our safe voyage. With my gifts of mangos, pawpaws and bananas, I sat on cases of champagne as we bounced in the small rubber dinghy towards the "Stormvogel." Dave and "WHN" were playing chase in the deep, blue water around the fabulous ship.

Before her chartering days, the "Stormvogel" won many very prestigious ocean races. Her galley was filled with awards and trophies as proof of her accomplishments. "Stormvogel's" crew consisted of Hermann as skipper; his wife, Paola, as first mate-hostess; two more Italians, Steve and Tika; and Ron and Pam, a young American couple, acting as extra crew, cooks, maids, and reggae music lovers.

On first introduction to the crew, I was disappointed— not that they weren't pleasant. Too many people, I thought...Why so many people? The Captain, crew, Dave, "WHN" and myself totaled nine. I'm greedy when it comes to islands; I like my islands to myself.

"We have good wind and two days of sailing to Palmerston Atoll; why don't we have lunch and be on our way," suggested the Captain.

Everyone agreed. We hopefully toasted to friendships, good weather, and the fulfillment of dreams.

"Any caviar? We can't have champagne without caviar," muttered guess who?

Dave laughed as I inserted a loud, "OH NO!!!".

"I'm sorry; but if we had known you wanted caviar, we certainly would have stocked it," said Paola apologetically.

I could see Paola was concerned about the request, and I felt a bit embarrassed.

"Pay her no mind, she's along to do laundry." I said.

"Did you hear what he said, Davy, dahlin'...Davy??"

Dave escaped with lunch and beer to the ship's stern.

As giant sails filled a cloudless sky, the Captain shouted orders in all directions. Paola held firm to the wheel and watched the compass. The crew wrestled with the wind in an attempt to hoist a colorful spinnaker.

It was a lot of work; from the time we raised anchor until we were well under sail, the Captain and his crew did not have a moment's rest. They were pulling on this rope, and fastening down that rope, checking maps, and listening to weather reports. Soon I realized why so many crew members were needed; this was not the 43-foot "Roscop" sailing from Huahine to Raiatea on a half-day sail. We were headed into the immense, boundless Pacific aboard 78 feet of ship, powered by a wind as unpredictable as a woman.

"Davy, dahlin', do you think they take American Express on Palmerston Atoll?" said "WHN" in a squeaky high pitched voice. Without answering, Dave rolled his eyes and moved to the bow, leaving me alone with his champagne-sipping companion.

"It's going to be a long trip, Joan; sit down here and let me give you a rundown on where we're going."

"Did I say something wrong? I never leave home without it."

"Joan, on Palmerston Atoll, there is a population of sixty. There are no roads, no cars, no restaurants, and no shopping malls."

"No shopping malls?" she said in disappointed amazement.

"You heard right. There are also no telephones, no beauty salons, no nothing...just coconuts, sand, sun and lots of interesting history."

William Marsters arrived there in the 1860's, with three wives to run a copra plantation. With the trio of wives, the Englishman produced numerous children; they married, and they produced still more children, and so on and so on...totaling today some 5,000 Marsters descendants. That figure is debatable, for I have read it could be as many as 8,000 scattered around the Pacific. The small population living on Palmerston have split themselves into three separate villages...a coconut's throw from each other.

The sale of copra (dried coconut meat) and fish provides the only sources of income on this lonely atoll, consisting of some 35 islands (only six of those are of any size).

Palmerston's remoteness and small population makes any type of communication here rare. The copra boat stops by reluctantly four or five times a year. There is little anchorage, and at low tide, the lagoon is completely closed by the exposed dangerous reef.

"Why in the world are we going there?"

"Why? WHY NOT...because it's remote, it's out there in the vast South Pacific...it's an island, an island that very few people in this world have ever visited."

"No restaurants, nightclubs, shopping...What are we going to do?"

"Who knows? Who cares?...We might be lucky, hit the reef, and sink. Then we're stuck until the next coconut boat visits. Wouldn't that be great?" I said seriously.

"Oh my...Oh no...don't even say that; don't joke around like that."

Joan, in her early thirties, sells real estate for a living at the opposite end of the world...New York. An attractive lady with long blondish hair and big green eyes, from the moment she joined us she seemed constantly in a high spirited jolly mood.

Did I say constantly?...

Right in front of my eyes she started to turn green. The mixture of champagne, lunch, Palmerston stories and—most of all—the rolling sea did her in for the rest of the day. She retired to the bathroom, not to be seen again until land was sighted, 210 miles of ocean later.

As we neared Palmerston, the low lying islands looked like green pimples on the face of the ocean. Through binoculars we spotted several small aluminum boats, filled to capacity with islanders racing in our direction.

"Hello. Welcome to Palmerston," shouted a young stocky islander, bobbing-up and down in his silver craft. "Good day; I'm Captain Hermann and I have charter guests who would like to visit your island for a day or so."

"That would be nice...we see very few visitors. I'm Melbourne Marsters. This is George Marsters and my girl friend, Akera Marsters. We need to check your papers please."

As my Minolta cranked from frame to frame...I thought to myself...formalities, formalities, even in this remote spot.

"Look at his T-shirt" whispered Dave, pointing towards

Melbourne.

"Oh No...No... I can't believe it."

"What is it?" said "WHN."

"Read it," I said.

"MICHAEL JACKSON—THRILLER. I like Michael Jackson...what's wrong with Michael Jackson??"

I wasn't about to explain...She would never understand. Aluminum boats with Yamaha engines...instead of outriggers; a Michael Jackson T-shirt, instead of bare chests and flowers...no, she would never understand.

The moment Melbourne and his crew boarded, the other boats made a U-turn in a direction back to Palmerston. I had heard and read that the three different families there do not like each other: they don't share, they don't speak, and they even load copra sacks on different sides of the cargo ship.

George Marsters checked the documents (very slowly), consuming several cold beers (rare on Palmerston) in the process. Melbourne eyed my guitar and motioned to have it passed his way. We were more than eager for some Cook Islands music...so as sails were lowered and Palmerston grew nearer, Melbourne sang...

THERE'S A PLACE, THAT I RECALL
IT'S NOT TOO BIG, BUT IT'S KINNA SMALL
THE PEOPLE THERE LOVE THE ISLAND ALL
A SIMPLE LIFE FOR ME,

SO COME ON DOWN TO PALMERSTON
LAY DOWN ON THE BEACH
SUNNY DAYS AND THE MOONLIGHT NIGHTS
IS WHERE I USED TO BE,

THE COCONUT TREES ARE NEARER
STANDING ALL ALONE
THE MAGIC OF THIS HAPPY LIFE
IS CALLING ME BACK HOME

Melbourne's deep, crisp voice was enriched with Akera's harmony, as she swayed to the soft strumming of the guitar. Her slightly plump, brown body moved about the "Storm-vogel's" cockpit, then George Marsters joined in the singing...

WHEN I WAS YOUNG AND NOT TOO SMART
I LEFT MY HOME FOR A BRAND NEW START
TO FIND A PLACE
THAT IS BETTER STILL
BUT NOW I KNOW
THAT I NEVER WILL,
SO COME ON TO PALMERSTON...LAY DOWN ON
THE BEACH...

The dancing and singing, mixed with the panorama of Palmerston's tall coconut trees, sandy shore, and thatched huts, was some enchanting sight after several days of endless ocean.

A two mile walk around the main island took no time at all, and we saw all the points of interest: the old wooden church, the schoolhouse, the one-seater outside bar with no booze, and William Marster's grave.

That evening Akera cooked a cake made from the soft interior of sprouting coconuts, mixed with sugar and flour. John Marsters, father to Melbourne and head of their family, captured several nice crays (lobsters). This, along with rice and steamed fish, made a great dinner; but we did find it awkward eating with fingers. Watching Joan nibbling on a fish head, while sucking bits of coconut from her artificial fingernails was an amusing sight.

Ignoring her request for eating utensils, I turned to Akera and said, "This is some fabulous dinner you made for us."

"For you...?? We eat like this every day," said John.

"Yes. We do not have much on Palmerston, but we always eat well," added Melbourne.

After dinner we made our way back to the lagoon. Captain Hermann gave a concerned look at the shifting wind.

"Just stay with us for the night." suggested Melbourne. Everyone turned down the offer as nicely as possible, but not I; I was more than anxious to sleep on an atoll.

People on Palmerston speak English very well. In many ways they are much like the people of Pitcairn Island*, where there's a mixture of English and Polynesian blood. We exchanged songs and stories as the disappearing sun silhouetted the small thatched huts along the shore.

John proudly showed me his collection of VHS tapes.

"We should get a video player on the next ship," said John.

"So you're going to have video on Palmerston; that's no good, John."

"Why do you say that? We are looking forward to some good American cowboy movies."

"Well, John, I'm no psychiatrist, but take my word for it...you don't need television on Palmerston."

"Television? Oh it will be some time before we can afford a television; right now the video player and tapes are the best we can do."

What a relief, I thought.

Children of all ages and sizes laid on mats around the cement floor. John's house was small and simple, made of cinder block and a tin roof. A kitchen, eating area, and sitting

---

* Pitcairn Island is where the mutineers of the famous "HMS Bounty" settled.

room made up the main house, with the most modern appliance being a large deep freeze to hold frozen fish. The island's small generator is turned on several hours a day at different times, to keep the fish from thawing.

During our talk, the lights went off every 15 minutes or so. John would mumble to himself, get up, unplug the freezer, wait for the lights to go on and then plug it back in again. This seemed very routine for John.

He explained, "Whenever someone on the island plugs in an extra tape deck or turns on too many lights, this happens."

"I hope none of the other families have placed orders for new freezers...our small generator cannot handle it," said Melbourne.

"Talkin' about other families, where are they?" I queried.

"Oh, the men are on the reef tonight fishing, and children and wives are home."

"Yes, but John I'm told sixty people live on this little island...I've seen only your family; where are the rest?"

Melbourne changed the subject..."Tomorrow, you and I will go in the lagoon; we'll get some crays, fish and crab."

"That sounds great, maybe we can get the rest of the Islanders to join us for a party."

"All your friends on the ship should come, and our family; that would be plenty," injected John with a slight command. "The girls will prepare more food than you can imagine so, you have the Captain bring rum. We ran out long ago."

The following morning brought bad weather. Tall coconut trees bent with the direction of near gale winds, and the sea beyond the reef turned into a convulsion of rampant white caps. While I was chomping on my breakfast of fish and coconut cakes, Dave brought the bad news.

"Let's go, George; there's a dreadful storm coming, the

anchor's dragging, and the Captain says we must sail."

"Dave, we've got a big feast planned for tonight; the weather will clear up."

"Look, let's not argue about this; the Captain wanted to leave last night but stayed on so you could overnight on the island."

"The weather's bound to clear. Right, Melbourne? Tell him."

Melbourne looked out at the gloomy, gray sky and responded with a simple, uncertain, "It could."

"The Captain is the boss. He's not always right...but he's always the boss; let's go."

The Captain was right. As Palmerston disappeared in a pounding rain, we bobbed and rolled in mountains of the mighty Pacific, like a toy ship.

"You best get to your cabins, and fasten your gear down. I hear things flying around down there," ordered the Captain.

On hands and knees, as the sea crashed around us, I struggled to make the short distance from the cockpit to stern, and down a ladder to my cabin.

I received several, powerful douses of ocean along the way; and if that wasn't enough, my portable tape deck almost did me in as it flew across the cabin, meeting its shattered end against a brass porthole.

The small cabin looked as if a cyclone had been trapped inside, trying to make a desperate escape. Books, cameras, passport, snorkel, fins, film, anything that wasn't tied down (nearly everything) had found a new resting spot.

I tucked camera and passport under my pillow and left the rest, figuring I'd best attach myself to a bunk before ending up like the demolished tape deck. Waves and wind had no mercy on the "Stormvogel" and I found it difficult lying on my back, stomach, or side. Nothing seemed to work. I felt like pizza dough being rolled and tossed about in my unstable cabin. Once my somersaulting body got used to it, thoughts of Palmerston filled my head.

Why did the families not associate with each other? In a spot so remote, a place where ships rarely call, why did only one-third of the population come out to greet us?

Gee, I hope John was not too disappointed that I never found him to say goodbye. Akera's coconut cakes...MMM they were delicious. Fishing in the lagoon with Melbourne...that would have been fun.

Through constant pounding of sea against the ship's hull and the whistling wind through the riggings...surprisingly, I went to sleep.

A full day had passed, and so had the storm. I had missed several meals, daring not to attempt the short journey to the galley or to agitate a stomach that so far had kept its contents. Captain Hermann was playing with his charts and other navigational contraptions while Paola steered towards Suwarrow, a day's sail away.

"Well, how are you? Haven't seen you in a while," said Paola.

With unmistakable fabrication, I answered, "Perfect... couldn't be better."

"You missed a very good spaghetti dinner last night."

"Dinner? How in the world did you manage to eat through that beating?"

"Obviously you're not a sailor; that was a mild storm."

"Mild? Oh yeah, how's 'What's Her Name'?"

"She's still looking for her stomach in the forward bathroom."

"And Dave?"

"He hasn't missed a meal. In fact, he's in the galley right now having lunch."

I'd almost forgotten, Dave is an ex-sailor who had spent many years fishing the cold, hostile waters off British Columbia.

The sunset that evening was a fabulous display of broken clouds, bright orange and a calming sea. The horizon seemed to paint a message...there's good weather ahead.

During cocktails the following day, poor Joan made her first appearance in almost forty-eight hours, looking ten pounds lighter and several shades whiter. We greeted her with a big round of applause.

"Joan, want some champagne?"

She paid my ridiculing remark no mind and propped herself at Dave's side.

We were now having a leisurely, wonderful (though still a bit rocky) sail. Everyone was ready for calm anchorage inside Suwarrow's lagoon.

Suwarrow (sometimes spelled Suvarov) is the only atoll, besides Penrhyn, in the Northern Cooks offering a safe channel, enabling ships to enter its lagoon. To an island connoisseur, Suwarrow offers loads of interesting tales of buried treasure, great hurricanes, and beachcombers.

In 1942, a hurricane literally washed away sixteen of the atoll's twenty-two islands. During that violent storm, four small children and their father, Robert Dean Frisbie, a legendary writer of the South Seas, populated Anchorage (Suwarrow's main island). Fortunately, Frisbie tied his children to tamanu trees, bendable enough to withstand the flood of water and wind that doused the half-mile long island. They survived the great storm, and after their departure, a few coast-watchers were stationed on Suwarrow during World War II. They'd keep track of passing planes or ships; and by radio, they would relay air and sea traffic to allies of New Zealand. After that, the atoll remained uninhabited until October 1952.

That year New Zealander Tom Neale persuaded the captain of an out-island freighter to leave him and his cats on Anchorage. No, Tom wasn't mad, nor was he running from a wife or the law; he was just simply fulfilling a dream...that tropical dream of living alone, on your very own sundrenched coral island. Tom lived in lone isolation until he died in 1977. During this time he went back to Rarotonga on several occasions, but always returned to "his island."

As mentioned before, I've read Tom's book, AN ISLAND TO ONESELF, over and over again. The binding is falling apart and the pages are dog-eared; but for this Tom Neale groupie, the book is TREASURE ISLAND, MUTINY ON THE BOUNTY, and ROBINSON CRUSOE all wrapped up in one great publication.

As Suwarrow came into view, I held one hand on the bow's railing and Neale's book in the other. On page eight of the book, there's an illustrated map. I wanted reconfirmation that we were truly here, that the green specks in the distance were really the motus of Suwarrow. There's no describing my feelings as we inched our way through the pass. Neale put it this way...

"The only sound the lapping of the water and the creaking of wood, shading my eyes until at last I caught my first glimpse of Suwarrow. The pulsating, creamy foam of the reef thundering before us for miles, and a few clumps of palm trees silhouetted against the blue sky, the clumps widely separated on the islets that dotted the enormous, almost circular, stretch of reef. The air was shimmering and the sun already harsh as Anchorage started to take a more distinct shape. I could make out the white beach now..."

We had company in the calm lagoon, a schooner half our length was anchored about one hundred yards off Anchorage.

As we dropped our anchor, the schooner raised his. It made way towards the pass, then steered northwest in the direction of Samoa. Noticing the German flag on its stern, I thought to myself...*Good, there's room for only one Kraut on this island.*

Like a child on Christmas morning, the overwhelming excitement of being within swimming distance of Tom Neale's island had me bubbling over. I couldn't wait for the dinghy to be lowered; I dove in and swam for shore. Dave and Joan (back to her lively self again) followed. To our surprise, three Cook Islanders greeted us as we neared the beach.

"Good day; welcome to Suwarrow. Do you have your documents?" said the apparent leader of the trio.

Now this was some letdown, some slap in the face, disenchantment beyond disillusion. Isn't there some island left where regulations and bureaucracy just don't exist?

Dripping wet, huffing for breath, and trying not to laugh at the silly, yet disappointing question, I said in a jesting tone, "Dave, you did bring the passports didn't you?"

Patting the pockets on his drenched shorts, Dave said, "Not I; that's Joan's responsibility."

Joan, not catching on to our sarcasm, got a bit upset. "Passports? You guys said nothing about passports. Damn...let me rest a few minutes and I'll swim back for them."

The islanders put instant smiles on their faces; they must have found us amusing...or maybe it was the sight of heavy breathing, bikini clad, bosomy Joan.

We introduced ourselves. In hard-to-understand English, they did the same.

"I Jimmy Tangi fom Manihiki."

"I Daniel fom Manihiki."

"An' I Rolan' fom Raro."

"You maybe like fresh coconut water?" asked Daniel.

"Sure, that would be nice. What are you fellows doing here

on Suwarrow?" inquired Dave.

"We watch coconuts and build stone dock," said Roland.

"LOOK OUT!" screamed Joan.

With a big "THUMP," a half dozen green coconuts dented the sand between us. We looked up in a maze of swaying fronds. There was Daniel some eighty feet up grinning, waving, and shouting..."Here come more."

"THUMP"—"THUMP"—"THUMP."

Daniel chopped open the nuts as fast as we could down the refreshing drink. In a shady forest of coconut trees, the islanders did their best to explain "coconut watching."

Termites had been found in some coconut trees on Suwarrow. So what, you say? Well you see, the sale of copra (dried coconut meat) is the main economy of many islands in the South Pacific. Copra is exported and then used for making oils, cosmetics, soap, and other products.

Now, when not exported, the coconut has endless uses for the islanders.

The fruit (the coconut) is an important ingredient in many island recipes including cakes, drinks, puddings, and fish. Coconut oil is used in the hair as a conditioner, for the skin as a lotion, and in the frying pan for fish. The tree trunk is used for building huts and canoes. Fronds of the tree are used to make hats, baskets, fish traps, and roofs. To keep mosquitoes and sand flies away, the husk is burned, creating a thick long-lasting smoke better than most commercial insect repellents. The shell of the coconut can be carved into bracelets or earrings for selling to tourists. And probably most important of all, the coconut water can be a life saver on a dry, often rainless, atoll.

In Oahu, Hawaii I had once heard about six American airmen flying over the Pacific during WW II. They had engine trouble, causing them to bring their monstrous cargo plane down in the mid-Pacific. Safely they landed in the lagoon of some remote atoll. It was many months later when a rescue team found them, or should I say what was left of them—six skeletons. Now had this happened to any Polynesian, a fast climb up a coconut tree would have meant survival for an indefinite period.

For one who immerses himself in island dreams, the coconut tree is symbolic of paradise. There is nothing more beautiful than the sight of palm fronds silhouetted by a full moon, swaying with the tropical trade winds. Coconut trees and tropical islands go together like...like...rum and coconut water (MMM good).

So Jimmy, Daniel and Roland make sure no fresh coconuts leave the atoll. This prevents the nasty, destructive termites from making their way to other islands. Daniel karate kicked a tall coconut tree; its eaten-out hollow trunk came crashing down.

"See, termite very bad for coconut," said Jimmy.

"Amazing...let me try that," I said.

In Bruce Lee fashion, complete with screams of, "SUUUKIIIAAAKIII, AAAEEEEEEAAA"...I clumsily flew through the air, in a collision course (feet first) with the nearest coconut tree. The tree stood firm, solid as concrete. With knee joints relocated in my hips, I crumbled to the ground with an embarrassing awkward, shamefaced "CRASH."

"Most trees still good on Suwarrow," said Roland, over laughter that echoed through the Cook Islands.

When not coconut watching, work on a coral dock was in progress. This small dock made of coral stones has been under construction since before the World War II coast-watcher days. Tom Neale also rebuilt the dock, only to have it washed away again by a sudden storm. Jimmy Tangi, the foreman of the trio, claims his dock will last; this is the first time cement was used to support its strength. That's questionable, though, since hurricanes have washed away entire islands on this atoll.

I was fascinated with the three islanders.

"You guys are so lucky; I'd like to be a professional coconut watcher."

"No lucky. Ship was come last week, now Raro (Rarotonga) radio us...maybe two more weeks for ship," said Roland somberly.

"New coconut watchers to come, but Raro say must wait," added Jimmy.

Daniel, looking unconcerned about the overdue ship, said, "I like Suwarrow, only miss women."

Jimmy and Roland nodded in agreement, turning their heads simultaneously in the direction of Joan, bent over collecting shells.

While Dave and the islanders made small talk, I walked up the narrow coral path to Neale's shack. This was castle to the "king of beachcombers"...more of Neale's pages flashed through my mind.

> "I pushed open the front door. Oddly, this act gave me a curious sensation, an almost spooky feeling as though venturing across the threshold of an empty, derelict building which held associations I couldn't know anything about. As though, in fact, I was trespassing into someone else's past which had become lost and forgotten, but was still somehow personal because the men who had lived here have left some vestige of their personalities behind."

Tom, of course, was talking about Robert Frisbie and the coast-watchers who once lived in this ten-by-ten shack. As for myself, the spooky feeling, along with the sense of trespassing, overpowered me. I had read Tom's book so often, it seemed disappointing he wasn't there to greet me.

I was startled by Daniel's shout, "Come, let's get coconut crab."

Coconut crabs, the ugliest creatures in paradise, are also a tasty delight. They resemble a giant hermit crab—minus its shell.

Daniel seemed more than anxious to act as tour director. Grabbing a long flimsy pole, he motioned me to follow.

"You from America?" he asked.

"No, I make my home in the Cayman Islands."

"Cayman Islands? You have coconut crab there?"

"Small ones, that live in a shell. We use them for fishing."

"For fishing? We use this for fishing," he said hoisting the pole high over his head.

We walked along the blinding white beach where coconut fronds hung over the shallow tidal pools like green canopies. Daniel looked to be in his late teens. In extremely good shape, his bronze, fat free, muscular body lifted a giant rock with ease. He grabbed a coconut crab before it made its escape and demonstrated the proper way to hold the ugly brute.

"No touch these, take off finger," he said pointing to its giant pinchers.

Daniel picked up a thick stick and demonstrated the crab's strength. The crab held the stick firmly with one pincher and "SNAP", halved it with the other, obviously teed off at the invasion of his rock covered home.

A dozen giant coconut crabs later, it was now time to fish. We waded in shallow, enticing tidal pools as schools of blue and green parrot fish jetted around us. With almost unsportsmanlike ease, Daniel speared several large brightly colored parrots.

I remember Tom Neale having a few shark encounters

on this part of the island.

"Do you ever have problems with sharks, Daniel?"

"SHARK...Look behind," he said, pointing.

I turned just in time to see two gray fins cutting through the calm, shallow water. Daniel threw his spear. Like two giant bullets, the small sharks shot off in opposite directions. Humored by my leapfrogging over coral, Daniel said, "Friendly shark in Suwarrow."

"Friendly sharks...never heard of such a thing."

"Shark small—dey have plenty fish, no like white man meat."

Neale, who walked in these same tidal pools nearly every day, wrote...

"Without a moment's warning, three sharks were charging towards me. Each looked about three feet long—the type which thrives in comparatively shallow water. For a moment I was almost paralyzed and then instinctively I backed hastily out of the pool, banging the water furiously with my rod...."

We had some feast that evening; the dark blue crabs turned lobster red in the cooking pot. The speared fish were grilled, and there was plenty of cold beer. AAAAAHHH..COLD BEER; Daniel and Roland were in heaven. If Palmerston ran out of beer weeks ago...that means it's been months since there was brew on Suwarrow.

The Captain asked Roland why Jimmy wouldn't join us.

"Jimmy, he miss family in Manihiki very much; he wait by radio. Maybe dey can talk."

"He also have watch coconuts," added Daniel.

What a perfect evening: our ship anchored in the middle of the world's largest ocean, yet the lagoon was so still, so calm...like a pond near some country lane. And the moon looked as if it had been impregnated with every bit of bright yellow the heavens could offer. Daniel sang a haunting, yet beautiful, song of the islands. Roland joined him in the full-toned harmony that seemed so natural to all Cook Islanders.

We spent six fabulous days anchored in Suwarrow's multi-colored lagoon. Between diving, exploring the other motus, feasting, singing, and following Tom Neale's long gone washed-away footprints, this atoll cast an unforgettable spell over all of us.

Our island hosts bid us all a sad farewell, with gifts of coconut meat, fish, and a carved replica of the "Stormvogel." We left gifts of rice, coffee, diving masks, and a bottle of Russian vodka. Over the clanging noise of a rising anchor chain, I gave Daniel my diving knife. He had become a special friend, teaching me the art of pole spearfishing, coconut crab hunting, and what tree to judo chop and what tree to leave alone.

"Maybe you come back to Cook Islands. I be in Manihiki soon," said Daniel.

"That's our next stop, would you like me to give anyone a message?"

Daniel presented a letter, "Yes, please you give this to my father. He name Okatai Ronga."

I'm not much on goodbyes, so I said a lot of silly things as Daniel, Roland and Jimmy climbed into their small boat.

"Watch out for those coconut crabs...When I come back I'll show you how to leapfrog the coral...Bruce Lee was a wimp compared to you, Daniel...Bye...If you see Tom Neale's ghost, tell him we said 'Hi'..."

The green, palm-filled islands became smaller as the mighty Pacific rolled off our bow, reminding us we were no longer in the protection of Suwarrow's lagoon. On Anchorage's beach we spotted a lone figure waving frantically.

Looking through binoculars, Joan said, "Dave, I think it's

Jimmy."

"No way, that's Daniel," said Dave.

I took hold of the binoculars..."No, you're both wrong... that's Tom Neale."

We were slicing through the sea towards Manihiki, approximately 160 miles northeast of Suwarrow, and all seemed too perfect. Dave and "What's Her Name" were deeply absorbed in a game of backgammon, between sips of cold champagne. Captain Hermann seemed pleased with what he called "ideal sailing weather." The crew laid about the ship, in any spot providing rays from a South Sea sun. I had the stern cockpit to myself. With "Barefoot Man" music flowing through my walkman, I was half catnapping and half watching a troll-line. "OH WHATTA TIME WE'RE HAVIN"...Then disaster struck...

WE RAN OUT OF BEER!!!!!!

"How could we be out of beer, Paola? Didn't we start with twenty-five cases?"

"Yes, but you made too many friends on Palmerston and Suwarrow..." said Paola, looking very concerned.

"I've got lots of champagne," giggled "WHN."

Dave, too, seemed very concerned, "Maybe in Manihiki we can get a fresh stock."

"Dave, you heard the news from all the other islands; they haven't seen the coconut freighter in some time. Nearly 300 people live on Manihiki Atoll, so that means more consumers. More consumers means less beer."

Dave agreed, "That's a good point...oh well, we can always drink coconut water."

"I've got lots of champagne," repeated "WHN."

"Champagne, yuck!" I said with disgust.

"You've got no class, dahlin', no class at all."

Manihiki is made up of 39 islands. Its deep lagoon provides mother-of-pearl shells, and there are also two cultured pearl farms there. Pearl shells seem to be the island's main money maker. Manihiki free-divers can effortlessly descend down to 120 feet. Copra and some of the South Pacific's best woven hats, mats and baskets are also exported.

Our arrival in Manihiki marked the second visit by a yacht in nine months. So, of course, this was as good a reason as any for a celebration. When the islanders saw our sails on the horizon, preparations for the party began. Several small piglets were slaughtered, flowers picked, and ukuleles tuned.

Tall, lean Ben Ellis, the island's CAO (Chief Administration Officer) gave us strict orders.

"The party begins at seven p.m. sharp."

"Ben, do you have beer?" I inquired.

"Beer...we have plenty of 'home brew' but beer? That's joke...freighter that bring beer in Samoa for repair."

"Home brew? What's that, Ben?" asked Dave.

"Powerful drink we make from coconut water, yeast and malt. You drink...it like coconut fall on you head from Manihiki's tallest tree."

"I've got lots of champagne," said guess who?

"Champagne? You have champagne, here on Manihiki? You bring to party, and I find beer," said Ben, obviously very delighted.

Well, well...it seems that bubbly, sparkling, belching, over-priced beverage, and "What's Her Name" saved the day.

"Ben, the lagoon sure looks inviting; where's a good diving spot?" I asked.

"All lagoon good for diving, but you must ask permission to dive from Chief of Island Council."

"You're not the Chief?"

"I am CAO; I represent Cook Islands Government. Chief of Island Council...he represent people of Manihiki."

"OK, where's the Chief?"

"Maybe in Tukao," said Ben, pointing·across the tempting blue lagoon.

We could see a small cluster of thatch houses, nestled between a forest of coconut trees. In Polynesian, Ben shouted orders to a group of young boys. They hastily jogged towards shore, one lifting a boat engine on his shoulder while the other grabbed oars and fuel tank.

"Come, my friends, I must check fish traps near Tukao. You ride with me, maybe find Chief," instructed Ben.

While the boat was being prepared, Ben gave us a fast tour of Tauhuna, the main village. Curious brown-eyed children followed us along a coral path, with the sea no more than 200 yards on either side. Our official tour guide explained the pearl shell business.

The different families of Manihiki have the right to certain spots in the lagoon—sort of like owning real estate on water. The families dive their submerged parcel for pearl shells that sell (depending on the quality) for about $1.40 per pound. The shells are cleaned, sacked and shipped away, mainly for making jewelry. On the rare occasion a diver finds a natural pearl, then (again depending on quality) he can be rewarded with extra money.

There are also two pearl farms on Manihiki. One is owned by Tekake Williams, who holds the island's record of free-diving 180 feet. This, according to locals, was also once a world's record.

Pearl farming has become big business throughout the South Pacific. The delicate procedure of artificially implanting the oyster with the fragment that will become a pearl is a well-guarded secret. Japanese "surgeons" or technicians are paid highly for their skills. After surgery, the oysters are placed in an aquatic recovery room where they are watched and pampered. Approximately one-fourth of the seeded oysters produce a pearl good enough for marketing.

Manihiki certainly deserves its reputation as being one of the most beautiful atolls in the Cooks. It's starting to become difficult to find fresh words to describe these islands. What do I say that hasn't been said already?

If you've visited one atoll, you've usually seen them all. However, Manihiki and its inhabitants have their own special distinction. The children have slightly oriental features, blue-black hair and bronze skin; they are beautiful and plentiful. The women have all the features one expects of a classic South Sea beauty. And as for the men...I was expecting them all to have big round barrel chests, muscular legs, and diving goggles strapped around their foreheads. After all, that's the way I've always seen them in "National Geographic." The Manihiki male, however, does come in all sizes, shapes, and shades of skin color. I was not disillusioned with my visions of a classic pearl diver when Ben introduced chunky, beaming Mitua Pouri.

"You must be a pearl diver," I said.

"That I am, and also constable," said Mitua proudly.

"Mitua, we would really like to go pearl diving in the lagoon; if you're diving in the next few days, could we please join you?" I said, almost pleading.

"Of course; that would be nice, but you must ask Chief permission to dive in lagoon."

Breaking in on our conversation, Ben said, "Come...boat ready...we go find Chief now and check fish trap."

"I meet you on return from Tukao, and we dive today," said Mitua as he waved a goodbye.

"Ben, why would you need a constable on Manihiki?" asked "WHN".

"Home brew sometime make people go crazy."

"Is it true that if someone gets out of order they are handcuffed to a coconut tree for punishment?" I asked.

Ben just smiled a wicked smile and didn't answer.

Right smack in the middle of Manihiki's lagoon, there's an island about one-third of an acre in size. It is home for a few shrubs, a few coconut trees, a small stretch of beach and its own coral garden. We circled the island about three times in a matter of a few minutes. Ben went on to explain that this is where many locals come for family picnics. Too much! As if thirty-nine islands aren't enough...here is yet another island within this circle of islands.

I drooled at the sight, "Ben, can you just drop me off and leave me for good?"

"You must ask Chief," said Ben.

"Chief...Chief...Chief...WHERE IS THE CHIEF?" barked Dave.

During our search for the Chief, we stopped at the local version of a fish trap, a maze of coral rocks along the reef. At high tide the fish swim into the maze, not finding their way out again. Low tide allows the islanders to scoop out anything worth eating.

"Ben, I've got a letter to deliver, do you know this guy?"

Looking at the crumpled envelope Ben reads out loud, "OKATAI RONGA".

"You folks very lucky."

We looked at each other in wonder and I said, "How come?"

"Okatai, he Chief."

"Ha, is that so? Daniel never even mentioned that. Now can we go diving?"

"Still best ask Chief."

We found Okatai fishing along the lagoon's shore. He wore no headband of feathers or jeweled crown, nor did he sit on a throne. He did, however, don a smile as wide as the lagoon when I gave him Daniel's letter.

"Please, you must stay and have coconut water drink."

"Sure, sir, then can we dive in the lagoon?"

"You dive...now we drink."

"I guess that's an affirmative," said Dave.

As we quenched our thirsts, the Chief and Ben got into some heavy-duty Polynesian chit-chat. Eyes ablaze, grinning, and hands in motion, they did regular finger pointing in our direction.

The Chief, now looking more thrilled than ever, asked, "Who have champagne?"

"I do, I do," said "WHN."

"On Manihiki, you have champagne?"

"On the boat, yes, I have about four cases left."

"You bring to party tonight. We dance for you, we sing for you...you bring champagne."

Joan was delighted. "These people have class," she said, "certainly more than you beer guzzling gluttons."

Dave and I looked at each other...was she talking to us?

We met Mitua in mid-lagoon, adorned with diving mask, weights, and that consistent grin. He motioned for us to follow as he plunged from his small outrigger into the glassy-calm lagoon. We slipped into the warm water, looking for the lagoon's bottom. All I saw was deep-deep-deep. Just how deep? Well, I took a quick guess. In such clear water one can normally see bottom in depths of 60 to 90 feet; I saw unending black...so, I figured it was more than 100 feet. While Mitua inhaled to prepare for his first dive, I asked about sharks.

"Only friendly sharks," he said (seems I've heard that before).

Friendly sharks? He could see my puzzled look and added that the sharks in the lagoon were small and if they came too close..."we kick shark in nose." He left me with that thought, took hold of a lead weight, and made his first descent. I just floated and watched Mitua disappear in the dark blue, deep below.

For a few moments, my mind flashed back to an old brick library in Wilmington, North Carolina. As a young high school student, I would stop there almost every afternoon and lose myself in "National Geographic" photos and stories on South Sea islands. A 1967 issue on the Cook Islands, showing several shots of the Manihiki pearl divers, was one of my favorites. Now here I was, in the same lagoon. Unbelievable...talk about dreams come true...Thank you, tiki gods. Mitua's surfacing bubbles danced on my face mask, interrupting my aquatic daydream.

"Where is he?" I thought to myself. Nearly three minutes had passed since Mitua descended. Then I saw him. At first only the yellow rim of his mask, then Mitua's broad body came into view. Surfacing gracefully, he seemed to appear on film, running in slow motion. When he broke the surface, he never gasped for air, nor did he cough up sea water. He just had that unfailing grin on his face, and went on to explain how he makes about twenty dives per day.

Mitua tossed a few pearl shells into his canoe, filled his lungs with fresh South Pacific air and again disappeared in the depths of the lagoon.

We spent nearly an hour, awed at his free-diving skills. I tried a few descents myself, looking rather clumsy beside fifty-year-old Mitua, who left me bobbing back to the surface about one-third of the way down.

On our way back to Tauhuna, Ben continued with his guided tour:

"See here to the east, we maybe soon have airstrip there."

Looking at the gorgeous palm smothered coastline, I said, "Gee, that's too bad, Ben, that's really too bad."

He gave me a confused look, and I didn't bother to explain. Ben pointed into the calm lagoon, "Here, this Tekake Williams' pearl farm...you dive...but no touch."

"What if we see a big fat pearl bursting from an oyster?"

asked Dave.

"No disturb," cautioned Ben again.

Some 165,000 oysters were strung in what seemed to resemble rows of underwater fences. It almost looked eerie—something so well organized, numerous and endless submerged in about thirty feet of this warm, clear water. We snorkeled around the underwater farm for some time. I took an occasional dive to scan the lagoon bottom in hopes that some careless pearl farmer might have dropped a pearl or two...no such luck.

Later, back in the village sipping a little "home brew", we noticed it was nearly 6:00 p.m. Ben and Mitua excused us from the afternoon happy hour.

"We'll see you later at the party," said "WHN."

"You don't forget champagne," reminded Ben.

"You don't forget food...and beer," reminded Dave.

Ben didn't forget...what a spread!!! Fried fish, boiled fish, raw fish, coconut cakes, papaya, grilled fish, octopus, minced fish, bananas, rice, fresh bread, puddings, and a dozen dishes I can't pronounce. As we surveyed the island banquet, Ben's wife, a lovely, well-rounded, happy lady smothered us with fresh flowers. In her best English, she explained each and every dish and how it was prepared, seasoned and eaten. Wearing a colorful flowered shirt and several leis of yellow and pink flowers, Ben joined his wife on her fifty course tour saying, "My wife is best cook in Manihiki."

Mrs. Ellis shyly giggled at the compliment and whispered something in Ben's ear.

"Ahh, yes...you bring champagne?" asked Ben.

To Ben's delight we produced two full cases.

And to our delight, Ben produced a fridge full of ice-cold New Zealand beer. The food was spread out on brightly colored tablecloths in Ben's front yard. Just as Dave and

I were betting who would devour more this evening, two roasted piglets were added to the bill of fare.

Manihiki citizens started appearing from behind every coconut tree, sporting an array of flower designed dresses, shirts, and simple wrap around pareus. We were introduced to the postmistress, the head of Public Works, the doctor, the minister, and other local civil servants. Each "hello" rewarded us with more sincere smiles and floral leis. We were starting to look silly, adorned with sweet smelling flowers, stacked till only our eyes peeked over the blossoms.

We consumed food till our bellies could hold no more, then washed it all down with the strong New Zealand beer. Joan's champagne was a big hit with the islanders. Every sip of the hard to get liquid was discussed in Polynesian. The whole scene looked like some tropical wine connoisseur's meeting, with Joan acting as waitress, refilling glass after glass.

The moon found a perfect place between the swaying coconut fronds and became a natural spotlight for what I tagged, "The Manihiki Symphony Orchestra." Ben on guitar, Mitua on ukulele, Okatai on shark skin drum, and a half dozen handsome young island boys on an assortment of cans, hollow logs, and pipes made up the balance of the band. While they played, the postmistress danced. Her body flowed in perfect time to the soft, enchanting rhythm. The barefooted Manihiki beauty also translated the Polynesian lyrics and, with hand motions, played out every line of the spellbinding songs. They sang about the lagoon, the birds, the gods, and the dark mysterious waters beyond the reef. Every islander present sang. Their harmony was so perfect, so clear, it ran chills through my body on this perfect warm tropical night.

I had my turn on the guitar. "Any requests?" I asked.

"Bob Marley," shouted some of the young islanders.

This surprised me. The reggae king's popularity was certainly more widespread than I had ever imagined. I reggaed my way through every Marley tune in my repertoire. When I switched to something a little softer, Joan sang along and stole the show. To everyone's surprise, our champagne consuming companion had some lung-power and delivery. Good ol' "What's Her Name" was starting to appreciate the natural beauty of the South Pacific—minus shopping malls.

A perfect day ended too fast, as all days seem to in paradise. The following morning bright and early, I found Mitua in his one room police headquarters.

"Mitua, let's go fishing."

"No fish today. Sunday day of rest. Taboo to go in lagoon."

"You mean no one goes into the lagoon today?"

"Only Seventh Day Adventist...You Seventh Day Adventist?"

"No, I'm...I'm, well to be honest with you, I'm not much of a church goer."

"You come to church today; no fish...friendly shark not so friendly on Sunday."

Well that thought was enough to keep me out of the lagoon, but go to church?...I tried to excuse myself from going.

"Mitua, I've got nothing to wear."

"You look fine for Manihiki church."

"What? Shorts, T-shirt and barefooted?"

"Bare feet no matter to God; this important," he said patting his broad chest.

The fishing conversation turned religious. This was getting a bit heavy for me, so I told Mitua I'd be back later. I leaned against a coconut tree and watched a parade of Manihiki residents on their way to church. Mitua wasn't putting me on; some were barefooted and very simply dressed. The ladies, of course, wore a fabulous display of fine woven hats and cheerfully colored dresses.

The lagoon looked extremely inviting with the morning sun shimmering on its glassy surface. *I'll wait till everyone's in church, then I'll take my chances in the lagoon*, I thought.

My serenity was interrupted with a loud "THUMMPPP," as a giant coconut crashed a few yards from my resting spot. Looking upwards towards the coconut's origin, the blue heavens peeked through green fronds. Then, just as the ground stopped shaking, church bells echoed in the tranquil morning. I think someone up there was trying to tell me something. So, guess who, bare feet and all, went to church?

The service, and especially the singing, was delightful. I'm glad I went. This was the way church should be. No one took notice of my bare feet or T-shirt, nor did the preacher ridicule his congregation because of a near empty collection plate. I felt very good, very fulfilled, as the beautiful singing reverberated in the stone house of worship.

The balance of our three day visit to Manihiki was equally gratifying. We fished, explored, made many new friends and unsuccessfully climbed coconut trees. Ben somehow found a few more cases of beer for the last leg of our voyage, 680 miles to Samoa. While Captain Hermann studied his maps, the crew prepared sails and lines.

The "Stormvogel" was loaded down with islanders. We smothered each other in farewell hugs and again were adorned with necklaces of flowers and shells. As Dave, "WHN" and I waved a final goodbye, one last outrigger came to "Stormvogel's" side. I was passed a wrinkled brown bag. Inside were six mother-of-pearl shells and a note written in pencil:

DEAR FRIEND,
THIS NOT VERY GOOD PEARL SHELL, BUT

PLEASE TAKE IT AS OUR LOVE TO YOUR
JOURNEY TO OUR ISLAND, HOPE TO SEE
YOU AGAIN.
OKATAI RONGA
CHIEF OF ISLAND COUNCIL
TAUHUNA, MANIHIKI,
COOK ISLANDS

A letter from Her Majesty the Queen, on Buckingham
Palace stationary, delivered by the Prince of Wales in a gold
carriage with royal guards, would not have meant as much
as this scribbled note on coffee-stained notebook paper.

It took nearly four days to make American Samoa.
Several visits by playful dolphins broke the boredom of
watching an endless ocean. Rusted Korean tuna vessels,
the black murky waters of Pago-Pago harbor, and flashing
neon signs advertising Budweiser, made it all very clear...this
adventure was over.

People
Of The

South

Pacific

XI

Summing It All Up

Is there such a thing as a real paradise?

If you have an imagination and a lust to wander...you will find it.

Paradise is, however, in most cases in the eye of the beholder. Islands, sandy beaches, and coconut trees aren't for everyone...thank goodness. Some people are content with a weekend in the woods, parked at a crowded campground, roasting hot dogs on a chilly night.

In a book titled THE LAST PARADISE, Andre Roosevelt wrote about Bali: "This nation of artists is faced with a Western invasion, and I cannot stand idly by and watch their destruction."

This was in 1930...over half a century later people still visit Bali by the thousands and still call it paradise.

I often think about this as I idle at one of Cayman's two traffic lights. Scanning George Town, I see the invasion. People from all corners of the world are here invading this never-never land. I do appreciate them; they have become a backbone to the island's stable economy. Nevertheless, each outsider (myself included) brings a bit of his or her foreign ideology. And soon we have satellite TV dishes, Burger King, Pizza Huts and nasty, money-hungry taxi drivers giving a bad reputation to those truly hard working friendly island cabbies.

Fortunately, basic geography is far from the mind of most people caught up in their daily nine-to-five urban routine. And Edens like Manihiki, Rarotonga, and Cayman Brac are just silly sounding names to them. And that's just fine as far as this island-seeking emigrant is concerned. It leaves for me more empty palm-fringed beaches to discover, and more dreams to fulfill.

My search for paradise has been more than rewarding, not only from a visual sense...but from all the knowledge I've acquired from the islanders themselves. I've learned to dive, to fish, to build a thatch hut...but most importantly I've acquired peace-of-mind and an ability to be content with what mother nature freely offers...sun, sea, and sand.

Even Harry, whose day-to-day philosophy often still puzzles me...he, too, has given me important knowledge.

Where does a beachbumming minstrel go from here? I'll never tell. Tom Neale was in his fifties when he went to live alone on Suwarrow atoll. And that's a fantasy yet to be rendered...Tom knew he could handle the isolation, and he did.

Could I follow his footsteps and maybe write a sequel to AN ISLAND TO ONESELF?...I d   know. Tom never had a good wife, beautiful children, and Harry...I'd probably miss them all.

About The Author

H. George Nowak is the creator of several other books— THE CRUISIN BOOZIN SONG BOOK, THE PEOPLE TIME FORGOT, and THE ABC BOOK OF THE CAYMAN ISLANDS.

Known best of all for his music and some sixteen albums that are a mixture of Calypso-Country and Reggae, George (THE BAREFOOT MAN) Nowak lives in the small village of Breakers, on the island of Grand Cayman.

He still performs almost nightly in the Ten-Sails Lounge...That is, of course, when he's not off on some remote island spearfishing.

He is shown in the photo above with children on Palmerston Atoll in the Cook Islands.

Glossary

Archipelago - A group or chain of islands.

Atoll - Low lying island built up from deposits of coral. A classic atoll is usually circular shaped and encloses a lagoon.

Awrite - Alright.

Badda - bother.

Breadfruit - A staple food that grows on trees and is round in shape, green in color. It has a starchy taste much like a potato.

Bredda - brother.

Calypso - Great uptempo island music played by The Mighty Sparrow, Lord Kitchener, Tradewinds and the Barefoot Man.

Cay - A small island, usually off the shore or near a larger island.

Classic - This book.

Copra - The dried meat of the coconut used for making oils, cosmetics, soap, etc.

Crawfish - Lobster without the claws.

Dat right - That's right.

Dat way - That way.

De bigga da betta - The bigger the better.

Dem - Them.

Der - There.

Dey 'ave no - They have no.

Dolla - Dollar.

Doubloon - Spanish coin from back in the pirate days.

Ex-patriot - Foreigner from another country.

Flim - Film.

Ganja - Marijuana, grass.

Gossip - It's everywhere on the islands.

Greenie - Heineken beer in green bottle.

Hinano - Beer from Tahiti and her islands.

Home Brew - Intoxicating drink made from coconut water on Manihiki Atoll and I'm sure other islands in the Pacific.

Hot wid fiah - Hot with fire.

Im hab plenty - He has plenty.

IRIE - Good, OK.

Jawg - Harry language for George.

Lear Jet - Small jet aircraft used in most cases for private charters or personal use.

Lego - Let go.

Lei - A necklace of flowers or a necklace of shells.

Machete - Large sword-like knife used for cutting bushes and to break open coconuts.

Mah-Rhu-Rhu - Thank you in Tahitian.

Mel Fisher - Famous treasure hunter; very nice person.

Mohn - Man.

Muff Diver - Call your local dive shop to get this information.

Motu - Low lying small island.

Mother-of-pearl - The silver shiny part of the oyster shell that is used in making jewelry.

Nah-Nah - Goodby in Tahitian.

'Oliday - Holiday.

'Ow come - How come.

Pareu - Men's or women's colorful wrap-around skirt.

Penrhyn - The northernmost atoll of the Cook Islands.

Pina Colada - Great island drink made from rum.

Reggae - Music that originated in Jamaica, Bob Marley type.

Rum Punch - Island drink made from rum and a mixture of fruit juices.

Shooter - Hawaiian sling used for spearfishing. Can also be a shot of booze.

Tangaroa - A tiki god.

Turtle Burger - Same as hamburger but made from turtle meat.

Wahine - Woman.

West Indian - Someone from the West Indies or the Caribbean area.

"WHN" - What's her name.

Work Permit - Visa to allow one permission to work in another country.

"Yellow Bird" - Famous island song, very popular with the tourists.

ZZZZZZZZZZZ - Sleep, boring like this glossary that has come to an end.